Lt. Colonel Lyell M. Rader
May 1, 1902–April 28, 1994

Portrait of the author at age 25,
a newly commissioned lieutenant in The Salvation Army.

ROMANCE
&
DYNAMITE

ESSAYS ON SCIENCE & THE NATURE OF FAITH

Lt. Colonel Lyell M. Rader, D.D., O.F.
Foreword by General Paul A. Rader

*Compiled from articles first published in the Salvation Army's
USA War Cry and other periodicals*

Crest Books
Salvation Army National Publications
615 Slaters Lane
Alexandria, Virginia 22313

Published by Crest Books, Salvation Army National Publications
615 Slaters Lane, Alexandria, Virginia 22313
(703) 299–5558 Fax: (703) 684–5539
http://publications.salvationarmyusa.org

Printed in the United States of America

All photos courtesy of The Salvation Army National Archives and Research Center.

Layout and design by Jeffrey McDonald and Jennifer Davis Dodd.
Cover design by Laura Ezzell.

Library of Congress Catalog Card Number: 98-74550

ISBN: 0–9657601–5–4

TABLE OF CONTENTS

Foreword
Introduction

HINTS OF THE HOLY LIFE

MARKS OF THE SPIRIT'S SHARP SWORD

FOREWORD

My father, Lt. Colonel Lyell M. Rader, D.D, O.F., was one of God's originals. Aflame with a passion for God and for souls to the end of his days, he was, in the words of his son and namesake, "a Salvationist zealot." He lived and breathed his covenant as an officer in The Salvation Army—to make the salvation of the lost the first great purpose of his life. Few have pursued that calling with keener delight or greater intensity. He was without peer in personal encounters with the seeking sinner. He could virtually smell soul hunger. He had an uncanny sense of when persons were ready to move Christward in decision. He was unrelenting in his pursuit of those on whom he had fixed his sights in faith, no matter how stubbornly resistant they might appear. He could literally believe belief into the unbelieving. He had a way of assuming a faith and goodness in those he encountered that could be positively discomfiting to those who knew better of themselves. Often his confidence in them seemed to elicit an unexpected hungering and thirsting for righteousness.

His tenacity of faith in intercession for the most incorrigible of prodigals is legendary. Right to the final days of his long life, which ended just before his 92nd birthday, seeking the lost was his all–consuming passion. And not just seeking them. He was a discipler, sometimes investing awesome amounts of time and energy in carrying the weak and the wavering, as he sometimes put it, "piggyback to Glory." When he could no longer go to them, he entered upon a remarkable ministry of prayer and intercession that seems still to snatch them as brands from the burning.

His background in electrical engineering and his life-long fascination with the wonders of the natural world provided him with unforgettable examples of the Creator's hand and redemption's plan. Told in his colorful idiom, his lessons from science and the Bible were always compelling. Whether holding a large congregation spellbound in a citywide crusade, gathering a crowd of the curious in the open air—and few can have pursued that ministry with greater skill and effect—or stirring the imaginations of his children and grandchildren in family devotions, he presented the Gospel, often with an object lesson or remarkable evidence of God's loving design in the created universe, dispelled doubt and drew his hearers to saving faith, launching them into the "romance of a God–led life."

The chapters that follow pulsate with the passion of the evangelist and the guileless delight of one who never ceased to wonder at the glory of God revealed so dazzlingly in the created universe. He neither saw nor could conceive of any conflict between the Living Word, the written word and the natural world. These messages are presented as he wrote them and as he spoke them, with clarity and conviction, over the years of his ministry. Some may be inclined to quibble over details of scientific explanation in the light of current understanding, but the points to be made are unerring in accuracy and solidly grounded in both Scripture and experience. Nothing would give him greater joy nor more signally honor his memory than for those who pursue these pages to encounter in them the prior claim of Christ's love upon their total devotion and to respond to his call to holiness of heart and life, striking out with a bolder faith and firmer stride on the greatest of life's adventures.

General Paul A. Rader
International Leader of The Salvation Army
London, England

Lyell Rader Enters Heaven

And is he come, this mighty man of prayer;
This man of faith, this intercessor bold,
Who shared his Master's heart; expressed his care
Whose arms both saints and sinners could enfold?

Around him gather those his prayers have blessed,
And those for whom he has a special love,
For Lyell has entered his eternal rest,
The man of faith below, now "faiths" above.

And is he gone, this man who spoke with God,
Whose prayers brought strength, hope and grace to all,
Who, with his Lord, the path of prayer has trod
To aid the weak and lift up those who fall?

Now he is gone who then will pray for me?
Who bear me up to God's great throne of grace?
Who help me to keep my path from danger free
Enabling me in heaven to find my place?

Lord, raise up others who in prayer are strong,
Christ's ministry of prayer to reinforce,
To keep within my heart a triumph song,
And be a crucial influence on my course.

Commissioner Harry Read (R)

INTRODUCTION

My heart's desire was to make gunpowder. One day I found the door to my chemist father's lab open. I went in, found a book that looked like it might tell me what I wanted to know, and pulled the big tome off the high shelf. I've still got the book: Henley's *Formulae*. It had a lot of stuff that I wasn't interested in, like how to grow a thick moustache. I couldn't even grow a thin one back then. But, finally, I found the code I was seeking.

I cased the place for the necessary chemicals and found them. I had to burn matches to get the carbon. The directions said to use equal proportions of three chemicals, grind them with water into a paste, and then evaporate the water.

Well, I didn't want to spend all day waiting for the

water to evaporate. It didn't make a lot of sense to me to put water in if I were to just take it out, so I bypassed the water. I put the three dry ingredients into Dad's new marble mortar, and I began to grind. I say "began to grind" because I don't remember much after that.

When I woke up on the floor with Dad's shattered mortar all around me, I learned something about chemistry. When a formula says, "put water in," you'd better do it. In other words, don't fool with the formula. A lawyer can put his mistakes in jail. A doctor can bury his mistakes. A chemist often takes his mistakes with him. Fortunately, most chemists don't fool with the formula.

In this book are stories of God's creative marvels in nature, which have first been hammered home at the family altar, then at boys' camp, and, finally, on the evangelistic trail. They reveal a formula for life.

It is my hope that Salvationists—and all Christian parents—will find some grist for their own mills in grinding out family altar formats for their children that are both fascinating and faith building.

The Bible is not just a book for monks and missionaries. By living by it, every child can find the way to heaven. Nobody gets there by accident. This intricate world didn't come about by accident either, but by the infinite intelligence, infinite power and infinite love of our infinite God. Your children may be won to the Lord at the penitent form at the corps, but they can also be won right there at the family altar.

Use the family altar; get them thoroughly established on the Scripture. That is their authority. Don't let them just look back to a penitent–form experience. They've got to look forward and look up into Jesus' face and, through his word and the witness of the Spirit, be sure they're soundly converted.

Stay out of ruts. Keep the format varied. Keep it interesting, entertaining. Get them into the act–listen to their questions and to what their teachers or textbooks have to say. They may be giving the credit for all creation to Mother Nature rather than to Father God, to evolution rather than to creation.

Arm your children with "thus saith the Lord." Let them know where the battle lines are drawn, that the god of this world is the devil. It is an evil world. Saint Paul said, "The world has been crucified to me, and I to the world" (Galatians 6:14). As Christians, that should be our attitude as well.

Ephesians 6:10–13 warns us: "Be strong in the Lord and in his mighty power. Put on the full armor of God so that you can take your stand against the devil's schemes. For our struggle is not against flesh and blood, but against the rulers, against the authorities, against the powers of this dark world and against the spiritual forces of evil in the heavenly realms. Therefore put on the full armor of God, so that when the day of evil comes, you may be able to stand your ground, and after you have done everything, to stand."

Every item of God's armor fulfills a different function of the Bible in a believer's life, protecting God's child from Satan's onslaughts of temptation (Ephesians 6:14–18). "We know that we are children of God, and that the whole world is under the control of the evil one" (1 John 5:19). Therefore, teach your children never to be impressed with majority opinion. Nearly every scientific breakthrough showed the majority opinion about the outcome to be wrong.

Christopher Columbus was alone in his belief that the earth was round, when most educated, well-informed people believed it was flat. Alexander Graham Bell was thought to be ridiculous in claiming that he could send a message over a wire, but we all hail him now as the father of the telephone. Thomas Edison was despised when he invented the electric light. Nobody came to his grand opening, and he had to hang the thing out of the window for the world to see before, one at a time, erstwhile skeptics came ashamedly to examine the invention. Then they predicted it would burn out. But it didn't. Now we hail him as the father of the electric light (and the phonograph).

Henry Ford was called an old fool when he claimed he could put a yellow powder, chrome, in steel so it could get hot without losing its temper, but he made a fancy fortune out of his Tin Lizzie. The first steamboat was called Fulton's Folly, but it worked, and ushered in the steam age.

Westinghouse was laughed to scorn for saying that he could stop a long railroad train with wind. Yet Westinghouse airbrakes are still in operation, while all of the critics are dead. As God says in Isaiah 55:8–9, "'For my thoughts are not your thoughts, neither are your ways my ways,' declares the Lord. 'As the heavens are higher than the earth, so are my ways higher than your ways and my thoughts than your thoughts.'"

So when our children would explode with, "Gee, Dad, all the kids ... " I would stop them right there and say, "Never mind what all the kids say or do. Let's see what God almighty has to say." Then we would turn to the word of God and discover the mind of Christ.

This doesn't mean that we didn't listen to the kids. They had their say—indeed they did—and we listened to their objections. But our answer was always to lead them back to the Bible to see exactly what God had to say on the subject in question. Isaiah 54:13 says, "All your sons will be taught by the Lord, and great will be your children's peace."

Our first aim was the salvation and sanctification of our children. We insisted upon daily Bible study and memorizing great texts. I found a nice piece of hard wood, made little blocks and drilled four holes in each for four colored pencils, so we could mark our Bibles. The family had a lot of fun doing that. Red was for salvation verses, blue for holiness, yellow for prophecy and the second coming and green for promises.

Francis Schaeffer pointed out that "man thinks he is the measure of all things, that he is capable of correcting God." But God has other ideas. He reveals that man's mind and judgment can be badly warped by his warped and wandering will.

The only provision God has made for correcting this bent, this inclination toward evil in "the mind of the flesh," is "the washing with water through the word" (Ephesians 5:26). The blood forgives and washes guilt away. The word corrects our course. The word transforms "by the renewing of your mind. Then you will be able to test and approve what God's will is—his good, pleasing and perfect will" (Romans 12:2).

Part I:

Images of Salvation

Could deeper, higher wonder ever be?
That he, creation's king, for love of me
Once left his throne ineffable, and came
To hang upon a felon's cross of shame!

Or was there ever costlier purchase–price
Than that astounding, vast self–sacrifice,
To set a guilty sin–bound captive free,
and open Paradise, at last, to me?

J. Sidlow Baxter

ROMANCE &
DYNAMITE

Who would have dreamed that a garbage dump could yield perfume, paints of rainbow hue and power enough to blow heads off? Yet it is true. During World War I, when America was running out of raw materials, some chemists, in desperation, turned to the garbage dump for aniline oil, the base for perfume and paint.

At this time William Miles Hayney also recovered glycerine from garbage. Nitrating the glycerine, he produced nitroglycerine, the basis of dynamite.

God is at work in our human scrap heaps, too, for grace and for glory: "If anyone is in Christ, he is a new creation; the old has gone, the new has come!" (2 Corinthians 5:17). The alternative is for a person to "go from bad to worse, deceiving and being deceived," "being hated and hating one another" until he dies in his sins "without hope and without God" for all eternity—a fate too horrible to contemplate (2 Timothy 3:13; Titus 3:3; Ephesians 2:12).

In Philadelphia, years ago, a drug addict and alcoholic named Tony Zeoli was so familiar with the inside of Eastern Penitentiary that he almost felt at home there. His nickname was "the Terror of the Tenderloin" (the Bowery of Philadelphia). Back when a dollar was a dollar, he needed $300 a day to support his habit. That called for a lot of crime!

Tony was the black sheep of a lovely family. When his brother was about to be married, he confided in his wife-to-be that he had a brother in prison, a hopeless criminal. She opened her purse, took out a New Testament and said, "Give him this. Maybe it will help."

The prison guard threw it to Tony, saying, "Here, maybe this will do you some good." Tony picked it up, and it fell open to Matthew 24. His eye caught the 35th verse, "Heaven and earth shall pass away, but my words shall not pass away." He laughed contemptuously.

Later Tony approached a couple of inmates who were loudly witnessing to their newfound joy in the Lord. "Look," he told them, "you say this is God's book. Yet nobody but an idiot would say, 'Heaven and earth shall pass away, but my words shall never pass away.'"

"Yeah, if you or I said that, we would have to be

crazy," came the response, "but Jesus said that. He made it all. He ought to know when it's going to pass away. But let me give you a little promise your size." He turned Tony's new Bible to John 5:24 where Jesus says, "Verily, verily, I say unto you, he that heareth my word, and believeth on him that sent me, hath everlasting life, and shall not come into condemnation; but is passed from death unto life" (KJV).

The inmate went over it several times until light dawned on Tony. He especially liked the part, "shall not come into condemnation." Tony had faced condemnation all his life; whenever a crime was committed in the Tenderloin, the police always looked up Tony and frisked him for a gun or a knife or a needle. They were sure he must have had something to do with it.

But Tony objected to the last phrase of the verse, "is passed from death unto life." He said, "How can anything be 'is' and 'passed' at the same time? That's not even good English."

"Man, I don't know much about English," his fellow prisoner answered, "but I know Jesus, and when you trust him to forgive all your rotten sins, he does it so fast, they is passed!"

Tony responded, "If that's true, it's my only hope." Hurrying off to his cell, he fell upon his knees and cried out to Jesus to save him. He began reading the Bible and kept reading—through his yard time and into the evening, when all the cell lights went out. But there was still light on the catwalk outside. Tony got as close as he could to the door so he could continue to read in the light from the catwalk.

As the guard passed by, he noticed the back of Tony's head. "What are you doing, Tony?" he asked.

Recognizing the man who had thrown him the Testament, Tony responded, "You know the Testament you gave me? I've asked this Jesus to come into my heart and forgive me of a rotten life and be my Savior."

The guard started to cry and said, "You know, Tony, I used to know Jesus like that, as a boy."

"What! And you let him go? He's our only hope, man!" And Tony led the guard back to Jesus through the barred door of his prison cell.

Tony joined the converts in their prayer group and, happy in the newness of life in Christ, was noisier than they were.

Before my father heard about him, Tony had led three of the guards and six of his cell–mates to Jesus. Dad went to the warden and said, "If you parole this man, he can live in my home." For three months after his release, Tony was my roommate, and what a fellow-ship we had! Every time I wanted to loaf and kill time, he'd slap me on the back and say, "We're wasting time, Lyell; let's get on our knees," and we'd have a little prayer meeting together.

Tony attended Philadelphia College of the Bible to get a better understanding of the word. He excelled in memorizing Scripture and was soon known as "the walking Bible." He developed a ministry over Radio Camden and was much in demand as an evangelist. Then his son, Billy Zeoli, grew to have a mighty ministry heading up Gospel Films, making Christian movies for evangelism.

Never write any human being off as garbage. All they need to know is the expulsive power of a new affection. *The love and power of Christ can overwhelm and destroy anyone's love of sin.*

Mel Trotter was another personal acquaintance straight off the scrap heap of humanity. One day his wife gave him money to get a prescription filled for their dying baby. Mel got drunk on the money, and the baby died. When the neighbors took up a collection to buy shoes for the dead baby's burial, Mel went in as if to mourn, stole the shoes off the baby's feet and pawned them for another drink.

He loathed himself for this action so much that he went to the Pacific Garden Mission on Skid Row in Chicago. (My cousin Harry Saulneir, who ran the mission for 46 years, had retired and turned it over to his son, David.) Mel stood in the doorway; a meeting was going on. He yelled, "Will somebody come and get me? I'm too drunk to get any further." David came off the platform and helped him to the altar. After the meeting, Mel slept off his drunkenness behind the piano.

Waking up the next morning, he saw some of the

mottos on the walls—"Jesus saves," "Repent and be converted"—and recognized that he was in a mission. "I must have got saved last night," he concluded. "Well, if I did, I'm gonna make it stick."

Mel Trotter personally founded over 60 rescue missions. He practically pioneered the rescue mission movement in America. There were a few ahead of him, like Water Street Mission and the McAuley Mission in New York. Of course, The Salvation Army had been doing this for years.

I knew these men and longed to get into similar front–line trench warfare to prove the power of Jesus to save, as Mel Trotter used to say, from "the guttermost to the uttermost." If I had another 90 years, I would gladly spend them and be spent for God's service in The Salvation Army for the redemption of mankind.

William Booth commanded his troops to "Go for souls and go for the worst. Net the very sewers as moral scavengers. We want all we can get. We want the lowest of the low."

The Army still is in that business. There is no such a thing as a person too wicked to be saved. Just because a someone is living in a garbage dump, that doesn't make him or her garbage.

Garbage is just good stuff in bad company. Chemists can reclaim it for glory and beauty or they can make explosives that tear men to pieces. It makes a difference what process you go through.

"Death and destruction lie open before the Lord—how much more the hearts of men!" (Proverbs 15:11).

**Every Christian, sooner or later, must choose one of
two pains: the pain of a crucified heart
or the pain of a divided mind.**

Samuel M. Shoemaker

GREATNESS
IN MINIATURE

With a gracious Ph.D. as guide, we were touring DuPont's great chemical empire in Wilmington, Delaware. Upon entering the nylon plant, our guide beamed and bragged, "Here we have actually improved on God." I didn't respond at once, but waited until we had finished the journey. Then I inquired: "How many operations have we seen between the raw material and the finished thread?"

"Twenty-two," came the answer.

"Well, how long does it take to go through all of those operations?"

"Several days."

"And how many individual filaments are there in the finished thread?"

"Oh, just a single filament."

"It's truly wonderful," I observed, "but you say you have 'improved on God.' A common spider can make its thread in one operation instead of 22. It doesn't require several days for the operation, just a split second. By the time the thread extrudes from the spinnerets and reaches the hind legs, it is cured and can sustain its total weight. Furthermore, one single thread is composed of more than 1,000 individual filaments. That's why it dries instantly. Besides all that, a spider carries its factory, plus raw materials, in its own body."

"Well," he conceded, "perhaps we haven't exactly improved on God, but at least the ladies like it better."

"Okay! So the ladies like it better. But that doesn't detract from the fact that no man can equal God's craftsmanship and, particularly, his miniaturization."

The greatest miniaturization of all is that our God and Creator, whom "even the highest heaven cannot contain," could be laid in the slender arms of the virgin mother and in a manger cradle (1 Kings 8:27). The greatest craftsmanship of all is demonstrated when a repentant sinner becomes "saved, through faith ... not by works, so that no one can boast. For we are God's workmanship, created in Christ Jesus to do good works, which God prepared in advance for us to do" (Ephesians 2:8–10).

As John Wesley once said, "This Christian life is the life of God, lived in these temples of clay, on the level of miracle."

St. Paul wrote, "Therefore, if anyone is in Christ, he is a new creation; the old has gone, the new has come!" (2 Corinthians 5:17). The Lord Jesus said to a theologian of His day, "I tell you the truth, no one can see the kingdom of God unless he is born again" (John 3:3).

A chief warrant officer in the WACs (Women's Army Corps) wrote to me: "I am just 19 days old in the Lord, and I can hardly remember what my life was like before I trusted Christ. It seems incredible that God would accept my first feeble step of faith."

When God speaks in his word, a built–in resonance responds with recognition in the heart of his children. *God's word is self–authenticating.* Jesus promised in John 14:21, "He who loves me will be loved by my Father, and I too will love him and show myself to him." Jeremiah 29:13 promises, "You will seek me and find me when you seek me with all your heart."

It is a wide open door, friend, and God's last invitation appears in the last chapter of the last book of the Bible, Revelation 22:17: "The Spirit and the bride say, 'Come!' And let him who hears say, 'Come!' Whoever is thirsty, let him come; and whoever wishes, let him take the free gift of the water of life."

Open my inward eyes,
Teacher divine:
Spirit of glad surprise,
Within me shine;
Quicken my inward sight,
So that I see
Gleaming in the clearest light
Thy word to me.

J. Sidlow Baxter

PHONY FACES, CHEAP GRACE

I own an owl butterfly, which comes from Devil's Island in the tropics. It looks for all the world like a great horned owl, so birds shy away from it. There's a little harmless snake that looks, at first glance, like the deadly coral snake, but its colors are slightly different. The monarch butterfly is very bitter to a bird's taste. There is another butterfly that rides on that reputation. It looks enough like the monarch to fool the birds.

Nature is full of such mimicry. This is too purposeful and widespread to be the product of chance. It is God's clever design. Albert Einstein said about evolution, "When the Almighty created the cosmos, he didn't throw dice." In contrast, a comedian once said of the economy, "The minute a good product comes on the market, somebody thinks up how to make it a little worse to sell for a little less."

For every genuine Christian born from above and showing the fruit of the Spirit in Christlikeness, Satan coaxes a phony to go through the motions of being saved. He or she might even go to the penitent–form, pray after the counselor, and exhibit all of the proper externals, yet miss eternal life.

A convert in New York City's Times Square fooled everybody except my wife. When I asked him for his name, he said, "Joe Ogden." I wrote it down, but somehow it didn't look right; I asked him to spell it. He said, "O–d–g–e–n." I wrote that and then said, "That spells Odgen." Then he gave me a billy–goat laugh and spelled it correctly. My wife said, "Don't you ever trust that man. Any man who can't spell his own name correctly the first time hasn't been using it for very long!"

But Joe fooled the census board, and they urged me to enroll him as a soldier in The Salvation Army. He bought a uniform. I asked for his address, but he said, "I'm here all the time. This is my address." He even wanted to become an officer. But I discouraged him: "You're too old, Joe, and too brittle. You could never take the discipline." He exploded in curses and left. Sunday after Sunday he stationed himself at the front door of the church to mock and curse those who entered. Eventually, he disappeared.

Months later I got a telephone call. "Captain Rader,

this is Joe, Joe Ogden."

"Well, where are you, Joe?"

"I'm in the Tombs."

"The Tombs?"

"That's right; the city jail. I killed a man. I want you to come up and see me."

I decided to see the warden first. He told me that the name "Joe Ogden" was his sixth alias; no wonder he didn't know how to spell it. He was wanted for various drug–related crimes in six other states. The most recent was the murder of his companion. The boy had been shot through the temple, his corpse dismembered and shipped as silverware to another city.

Yes, the devil has his counterfeits. On the Judgment Day, Jesus will have to say to some, "I never knew you. Away from me, you evildoers!" (Matthew 7:23). But one doesn't have to be as vulgar a hypocrite as Joe to miss heaven. Even nice people can miss heaven by 18 inches—that's just about the distance between the head and the heart.

Head faith never saves. It's got to be "with all your heart and with all your soul and with all your strength" (Deuteronomy 6:5). Then Jesus made it tougher still. In Luke 10:27, He said, "'Love the Lord your God with all your heart and with all your soul and with all your strength and with all your mind' and 'Love your neighbor as yourself.'"

Remember Jesus' parable of the ten virgins? They all

were in the same place, waiting for the same lord. Probably all had the same wedding garments on, as was the custom in those days. However, only five of them made it through; the other five were phonies, and they were lost.

Too many have head faith and think that's all there is to being saved. They may be accepted into a church on a so-called profession of faith when it isn't life-changing Bible faith at all. No repentance, no obedience, and the same old life of self and sin.

We must repent of sin before it is possible to exercise saving faith. The Pharisees professed to believe the Bible, but they sure didn't live it. Jesus said to his disciples, "For I tell you that unless your righteousness surpasses that of the Pharisees and the teachers of the law, you will certainly not enter the kingdom of heaven" (Matthew 5:20). The Pharisees had plenty of head faith and outward conformity to the code of their crowd, but God demands we be conformed to the image of his Son.

Real salvation is life-transforming and self-authenticating. Jesus becomes gloriously real. He shows himself to us, just as he promised in John 14:21: "He who loves me will be loved by my father, and I too will love him and show myself to him." And "The Spirit himself testifies with our spirit that we are God's children" (Romans 8:16).

"And without faith it is impossible to please God, because anyone who comes to him must believe that he exists and that he rewards those who earnestly seek him."

Hebrews 11:6

PERFECT WISDOM
AT WORK

erching birds, such as the chicken and the canary, have three toes forward and one toe back. Climbers and creepers, such as parakeets and woodpeckers, have two toes forward and two toes back. They look awkward, but they work. Birds of prey—owls, hawks and eagles—have one talon forward, one back, one right and one left.

Perchers have only one tendon that controls all four toes. When they perch, this one tendon is pulled over the knee joint automatically, clamping all four toes shut like a vise–grip wrench. Only when their legs are straightened can the talons be released. This is a great boon to a bird asleep on a perch.

Creepers have two tendons. One controls the two front toes, the other controls the two back toes. Birds of prey have four tendons, each of which controls an individual talon.

Here is perfect wisdom at work. A chicken needs a flat foot most of the time to scratch for food. When it does perch, only one action is required: to lock on that perch. The woodpeckers and other birds which constantly creep and cling to the bark of trees would never make it with one tendon, but two are perfectly suited to their needs. A bird of prey needs four tendons controlling its four talons in order to clutch its prey.

Do you feel disappointed and frustrated because you can't keep away from sin and can't hold on to God? You surely don't believe that eagles simply wiggled their toes until scratching nails became curved talons and a single tendon became four! Neither is the answer to your dilemma to be found in rearranging the jigsaw puzzle pieces of life for yourself. A psychiatrist can pick you to pieces and rearrange your priorities a little more efficiently, but only God can put you together again.

There is hope when we seek the mighty Christ, conqueror of death. He is also the Lord of life as it ought to be. He loved us unto "death—even death on a cross!" that we may "participate in the divine nature" here and hereafter (Philippians 2:8, 2 Peter 1:4). Whatever God has made works and works well. When Christ makes a man over in the new birth process, man also works well.

**Christianity has its creeds, but it is not a creed ...
has its rites, but is not rite ...
has its institutions, but is not an institution ....
Christianity is Christ,
or rather our response to him.**

E. Stanley Jones

SYMPATHETIC VIBRATIONS

The mosquito is best known as a pest, but if the sound of its wing beat is mechanically reproduced beside a planted kernel of corn, the kernel will grow to full ear in half the time the corn grows under optimal natural conditions. There is evidently a planned connection between the sudden emergence of buzzing hoards of insects each spring and the bursting forth of the vegetable kingdom in green glory.

A banana plantation in New South Wales, Australia has discovered that bananas, too, grow bigger and better to music. Cultivators use a loud constant note, irritating to the human ear but pleasing to bananas, to stimulate their growth. To quote a portion of the news report, "It is giving results out of all proportion to the amount of fertilizer used."

A government scientist in the field of bionomics expressed to me his considered opinion that the wing beat of every flying insect is probably geared to the growth rate of some plant.

Sir James Jeans, the English mathematician, physicist and astronomer, wrote: "Everything in the universe is in a state of vibration." Some of the vibrations are causative. Other sounds are results, called sympathetic vibrations. The tines of two tuning forks will vibrate together or they won't vibrate at all. The one struck is causative. This instantly results in the sympathetic vibration of the other. If two pianos are tuned perfectly alike, strike any note on the one and its counterpart on the other piano will instantly vibrate, but all the others remain silent and still.

Strike a certain note on a cornet, and a snare drum in the band closet will go crazy. I've seen the quiet glow of a gas mantle flare six inches high at the sound of a certain note from my brother's violin. While interesting in instruments, vibration points in cars can be ruinous. For my old Model–T Ford, years ago, 26 miles an hour was intolerable. The car would shudder from stem to stern at that speed, but at 25 or 27 miles an hour things would smooth out.

For bridges, sympathetic vibrations can be calamitous. The Narrows Bridge in Tacoma, Washington was built by an idealist who carried the beauty of his mathematics too far. He tuned the cables of the bridge, and a 30–mile–an–hour wind played the tune and ripped the bridge apart. Newspaper accounts called the bridge "Galloping Gertie."

Before the time of highly mechanized warfare, military engineers required infantry contingents to walk, not march, across bridges, lest they unleash an enormous force of sympathetic vibration.

Resonant relays can be controlled at a distance by sounds one can scarcely hear. The television can be turned on or off, up or down and channel to channel by a remote control device that only emits soft sounds.

The phrase, "I just don't vibrate to him," is probably literally true. Why shouldn't even brain waves be in harmony and hearts beat as one? One dictionary defines sympathy as "an affinity or relationship between things so that whatever affects one similarly affects the other; a correspondence in qualities, properties, harmony; a compatibility of temperaments." Antipathy, the opposite of sympathy, is "a settled aversion, an instinctive or constitutional dislike; a fondness or predilection in the opposite direction."

Sympathy and harmony characterize a happy married life. *The Christian life is simply one of getting in step with God.* It's tuning up to his standards. His great causative voice that once burst the summit of Mt. Sinai into flame can catch any honest heart willing to vibrate to his truth and make it resonate in perfect harmony with his divine will.

However, a tuning fork out of pitch with itself will not resonate to anything or anybody; it is dead to all vibrations surrounding it. So, if you think God is dead, you are the one who is dead to God.

If you are out of tune with God, you have not availed yourself of the power that can be released in your life once God tunes you up. "Therefore, if anyone is in Christ, he is a new creation; the old has gone, the new has come!" (2 Corinthians 5:17).

Get on God's wavelength. "Anyone who believes in the Son of God has this testimony in his heart" (1 John 5:10). "The Spirit himself testifies with our spirit that we are God's children" (Romans 8:16).

In spite of his universal sin, man is still loved, because we cost him the most.

Anonymous

THE WONDER
OF WINGS

It is popular to believe that one day birds and bees got tired of walking and crawling and decided it would be nice to fly. Specific details are lacking, but the theory goes that they frantically beat their arms or legs until they formed wings. Then they just took off and have been on the wing ever since. But let's look into some details.

When a pelican flies it maintains an easy one beat per second flap of its wings. A crow does a lazy two or three per second. It's very comical to see a large crow being chased by a little red-winged blackbird. The poor old crow hunches forward, trying frantically to pick up speed, but he is no match for the speedy little dive-bomber on his tail.

A pigeon takes off scared, often clapping its wings steeply together both above and below its body. Ducks have a rapid but shallow beat so they can clear the water. A pigeon's beat wouldn't do for a duck, and an old crow would shake himself to pieces traveling that fast.

Hummingbirds are the fastest members of the feathered kingdom in this category. A ruby-throated hummingbird beats its wings in a figure eight no less than 3,000 cycles per minute. It is marvelously maneuverable, able to fly upside down or backwards, or hover motionless like a helicopter. It has a variable, even reversible, "prop." Just how did this fantastic little creature happen to evolve wings and the motor to beat them so fast, as well as the sensitive controls to vary the pitch of the wing and even reverse it at will?

Our heads really begin to swim when we pry into the insect world. A fast vacuum cleaner motor turns up to 3,600 revolutions per minute, but the honeybee has been clocked at 11,400 beats per minute. Again, the beat is in a figure eight. If you think this is fast, a mosquito beats its wings 35,220 cycles per minute—nearly ten times the speed of a vacuum cleaner motor.

Let's consider one more example. The wee midge (smaller than a fruit fly or gnat) beats its wings 60,000 times a minute, or 1,000 beats a second—again, in a figure eight. This has been clocked by a calibrated stroboscope. Not even the electrical impulse of nerves can account for such fantastic reciprocal beats. It has been suggested that the upbeat triggers off the downbeat. What about the other controls? How do you account for them? There is only one real answer—God.

Creation did not develop "from goo to you by way of the zoo," to use Harold Hill's memorable phrase. And there is infinitely less chance of any of us getting to heaven by our own efforts or our own righteousness than there is of producing functioning wings by flapping our arms. As Gregory Bateson, an evolutionist, sadly admitted, "Not even the element of time can complete that which has never begun."

We were born in need of a Savior; we can, indeed must, be born again if we would reach heaven (see John 3:1–8). Then when he calls or comes, we will soar "to meet the Lord in the air. And so we will be with the Lord forever. Therefore encourage each other with these words" (1 Thessalonians 4:17–18).

No! We won't need a single beat, but we will need a second birth.

**No man ever looked long enough
and longingly enough at the love story
of the Cross without faith resulting.**

Anonymous

THE EYES
HAVE IT

Eyes are like intricate locks, to which light is the key. Some eyes are built to see in daylight. Nocturnal animals see best in the dark, as they have infrared sensitive photoelectric reflectors. The mighty 200–inch "eye in the sky" telescope atop Mt. Palomar is built on exactly this principle.

Government scientists study the fantastic gear possessed by insects, birds and marine life so they can duplicate it electronically. A pit viper, notably the rattlesnake, cannot only see its prey in the dark but, with those pits, can tell the temperature of its prey at a distance. It can detect a difference in temperature of one thousandth of one degree Fahrenheit. In addition to that, it can see where the flesh is deepest and the blood supply warmest. It plans its strike accordingly, and therefore seldom breaks its fangs by striking a bone.

Since World War II, military rifles have been equipped for night fighting with the snooper scope and the sniper scope. "Snooper scope" is military slang for an invisible infrared searchlight beamed from under a rifle. The sniper scope is an infrared telescopic sight placed on top of the rifle's barrel. With the help of this rattlesnake–like equipment, even on the blackest moonless night, the landscape appears to be lit up by a shower of bright particles from an exploding star.

Today, many electronic companies have duplicated the rattlesnake's visual equipment for the blind. They place the circuitry in the handles of conventional white canes. A slender wire runs up the blind person's sleeve to an earpiece. There is no need to tap the cane; he merely holds it in front of him. Instead of receiving visual impressions, the signals are converted into sounds. Thus he can detect a wall on his right, a curb on his left or an obstacle in his way. With a sweep of his cane, the blind person can tell in which direction the traffic is moving and can even sense a Volkswagen 100 feet away.

A normal human eye can behold the full sevenfold spectrum of color, but most of the animal kingdom is limited in the ability to perceive color for the practical purpose of detecting food, flower or a mate.

The eyes of a mosquito are microscopic. Its first

thrust must be down a hair follicle, and, unfortunately for us, it never misses its target.

The human eye has about 137,000,000 photoelectric cells. If you had 137,000,000 marbles and kept putting one down every inch and a half across the United States, from the Empire State Building to the Golden Gate Bridge, you would have 10,000,000 remaining.

Multiply that number by eight and you come near to the billion photoelectric cells that God has placed in a single eye of the hawk or eagle. A rabbit in the grass at 1,000 feet appears as a blur to the human eye, but is sharp and clear in the eye of a hawk or vulture.

One species of fish has four pupils in its two eyes—two for seeing above the water–line and two for seeing beneath—because this little creature is prey to both birds from above and turtles from beneath. The whirligig beetle has similar equipment, so it can watch for predator or prey above or below the water–line. The common honeybee has five eyes: two large compound eyes for seeing in white light and three smaller ones for seeing in infrared.

Humankind actually has three sets of eyes: ones that can perceive visible light, "the mind's eye" that can feed the imagination and the eyes of the spirit, which can see further and penetrate deeper in eternal matters in the light of God's word than any amount of stimulation of our five senses.

We can read a book and be the same afterward. *But*

if we read God's word with open hearts and open minds, searching for the truth, hungering after righteousness, we become different persons.

"Therefore, if anyone is in Christ, he is a new creation; the old has gone, the new has come!" (2 Corinthians 5:17). Sins are forgiven and forgotten. Evil habits are broken. The eyes of the soul, blind up to that moment, suddenly see, and the renewed mind deeply desires to walk in that new light (see Romans 12:1–2; 1 John 1:6–7).

Are we really to believe that everything emerged by chance and accident under the amorphous force called Mother Nature? Better to trust Jesus, "the Lord of glory," with life in the here and now and in the hereafter. The great Creator came to be Savior. If you seek for truth, remember Jesus said, "I am the Way and the Truth and the Life. No one comes to the Father except through me" (John 14:6). He is as good as his "exceeding great and precious promises" (2 Peter 1:4).

Ephesians 5:14 commands, "Wake up, O sleeper, rise from the dead, and Christ will shine on you." And 2 Peter 1:9–10 warns, "But if anyone does not have [faith, goodness, knowledge, self–control, perseverance, godliness, brotherly kindness and love], he is nearsighted and blind, and has forgotten that he has been cleansed from his past sins. Therefore, my brothers, be all the more eager to make your calling and election sure. For if you do these things, you will never fall."

"I will pour out My Spirit on all people ....
And everyone who calls on the name
of the Lord will be saved."

Acts 2:17,21

THE
WELL-EQUIPPED
PEST

E very mosquito is equipped by God with a walkie–talkie that has a supersonic range of 150 feet. It may take several minutes for the first one to find you, but once the word gets around, every mosquito in the vicinity knows it, and you had better move along quickly.

But this is only the beginning of its fantastic equipment. Inside that visible beak, which is only its tool case, lie six exquisitely delicate surgical instruments: two swords, two saws and two soda straws. The mosquito's saliva has three properties: it is a lubricant, an anesthetic and a solvent. Furthermore, its eyes are microscopes. A hair on your hand looks like one of the redwoods in California to a mosquito; it can't miss.

One never feels that first delicate probe down a hair follicle. The insect's saliva acts as an anesthetic. Then it carefully reams out the hole with the larger lancet. Now the reciprocal saws go to work. This gets the blood flowing. Then the mosquito pumps its solvent saliva down one straw to dilute the blood and sucks it up the other straw—cream and sugar to taste.

This combination of fantastic equipment had to work the first time. There was no place for error. Equipment had to be coupled with the simultaneous know-how to use it and in the right order. The very first mosquito had to know how to spit down one straw while sucking up the other. The end result was to key the little creature into the delicate balance of nature, to allow it to make a contribution and, at the same time, make a living without threatening other species.

This is, in very truth, the handiwork of God. He never made a creature without the needed equipment to live and to let live. He never created equipment without imparting the intelligence to use it, called instinct. He never made a creature that, left alone, would become extinct or that would cause extinction. Man alone messes up the balance of nature.

Unfortunately, our nature is already messed up. *We don't have to do a thing outlandish to go to hell, just keep going with the current. We do need to be "born again" to get to heaven.* Our conscience knows it; the Bible explains it; and the Lord Jesus died and rose again to provide it. He saves all who call upon him in truth. If you have never done so before, call upon him today.

"And everyone who calls on the name of the Lord will be saved" (Acts 2:21). If that's true, nothing else matters; if it's not true, nothing matters.

Long my imprisoned spirit lay
Fast bound in sin and nature's night;
Thine eye diffused a quickening ray;
I woke; the dungeon flamed with light.
My chains fell off, my heart was free,
I rose, went forth, and followed thee.

Charles Wesley

The Correct Key

E very lock can be opened, if you have the right key. Older locks of the better sort have five tumblers and two wards. The modern lock invented by Yale has the same number in better form. The tumblers in this case are split pins of various lengths. The wards are projections in the keyway that block the entrance of 90 percent of keys.

God has wards too. He commands us to draw near with an honest and sincere heart.

But even after a key has passed the wards, that's not enough. Only the correct key, all the way in, will have notches of proper depths to raise each split pin until all five splits are lined up along the line of cleavage between this movable barrel and the rest of the solid cylinder. Then the lock will turn. *No matter how complicated the lock, the answer is a single key, all the way in.*

Our minds are created in five logical strata: imagination, judgment, will, affections and emotions. If this ideal order were always preserved, we would easily recognize the truth, approve the truth, do the truth, love the truth and enjoy the truth. But sin destroys this beautiful chain reaction.

Romans 1:21 says, "For although they knew God, they neither glorified him as God nor gave thanks to him, but their thinking became futile and their foolish hearts were darkened."

The imagination, like mental television, can snap from God's channel of truth to Satan's channel of lies. How can the judgment be sound when the facts are distorted? How can the will be confident when the judgment is not certain?

Romans 1:24 tells us: "God gave them over in the sinful desires of their hearts to sexual impurity for the degrading of their bodies with one another."

In other words, their will went wild. And verse 26 of the same chapter continues: "Because of this, God gave them over to shameful lusts." How can people form an affection for shameful things? Because sin is always highly seasoned and palatable—at first.

Verse 28 completes the complex: "Furthermore, since they did not think it worthwhile to retain the knowledge of God, he gave them over to a depraved

mind, to do what ought not to be done." Here they jus-
tify sin; they rationalize. Depravity reaches the depths
of the subconscious. These unreasoning attitudes and
emotions, once like fluid cement, become thoroughly
mixed and permanently set.

Romans 1:32 gives the sad epitaph: "Although they
know God's righteous decree that those who do such
things deserve death, they not only continue to do
these very things, but also approve of those who prac-
tice them." Thus man locks his own soul against God.

Man's heart is not only locked against God; man is
upside down. He may use his head to run his business,
but emotions dictate the whims and urges of his sins.
Affections supplant judgment in approving action, and
the will, poor as it is, dangles helplessly between dom-
inant won't power and feeble will power.

In that arrangement, God cannot get through to us.
We must go by facts, not feelings. That's why we need
conversion, turning right side up. God will not compete with Satan on the level of the emotions, but neither can Satan compete with God on the level of truth
and light.

As sinners, we all must face the truth and seek the
light. Conviction and repentance are faculties of judgment, not emotions. We must come as we are—with all
of our complexity, blinded imagination, biased judgment, paralyzed will, perverted affections and troubled
emotions. Jesus is all we need. He is the single key.

He is the Way, the Truth, and the Light, and—glorious
news—we can come to him now.

The roads we take are less important than the goals we announce. Decisions determine destiny.

Frederick Speakman

GRAVITY'S CENTER

E ver wonder why some things fall and others stand? Why, for example, doesn't the leaning tower of Pisa fall?

To put the law precisely, the center of gravity is inside the circle of its base. As the center of gravity extends beyond the circle of its base, anything falls. Now, if this center of gravity is raised by adding to the leaning tower's height, the center is now beyond the base and it falls, a firm law of static physics.

Let's apply this law to a bicycle wheel. With the center of gravity at its mechanical center, it cannot be supported by a handle threaded onto the axle. But if the wheel is in motion, it can be supported because a law of static physics has been superseded by a higher law of dynamic physics. At the birth of motion, new laws burst into being; old static laws vanish, and some go into apparent reverse.

We live in a dynamic world of invisible forces. Electricity, for example, can be generated by the motion of wires through invisible lines of a magnetic field—and what astonishing energies are released! But the motion is not the energy. Motion simply releases the energy. The wheel in motion becomes gripped by dynamic energy that keeps it from falling.

Just as the wheel has no energy of its own, so we can do nothing to earn our own salvation. We can't get to heaven by pulling on our own bootstraps. We can't keep ourselves from falling. The closing words of the Lord's Prayer put it right: "Thine is the power, and the glory." *The power is not ours, yet we can have it, if we place ourselves in the grip of Redeeming Power, which, in turn, can keep us from falling.*

St. Paul explains it in Romans 8:2–4: "Through Christ Jesus, the law of the Spirit of life [a higher law] set me free from the law of sin and death [a lower law]. For what the law was powerless to do, in that it was weakened by the sinful nature, God did by sending his own Son in the likeness of sinful man as a sin offering. And so he condemned [literally, overcame] sin in sinful man, in order that the righteous requirements of the law might be fully met in us, who do not live according to the sinful nature but according to the Spirit."

God has deprived sin of its power. Calvary love and resurrection life and power can make a standing saint out of any falling sinner, if he centers his life in Christ.

There are three basic laws of life, three things we must do to stay alive and healthy. First, when we are born, we have only six minutes to live unless we take our first breath. From that point on, wonderful automatic machinery takes over, and we keep breathing. Second, we only have a few weeks to live unless we can eat and retain food. Here, too, automatic machinery takes over, and appetite warns when to refuel. The third law of life is use it or lose it; in other words, we have to learn to exercise our capacities to survive.

This parallels the same laws that govern the spiritual realm. After we are born again, we still need to extend ourselves into the ways of truth to sustain the newly gained understanding of life from God's perspective. We need his word to give us light, and prayer to give us might. Then even the weakest child born of the Spirit can obey and walk in the light.

To keep on living the Christian life, we must breathe the breath of Heaven: "Prayer is the Christian's vital breath, the Christian's native air" (James Montgomery). Second, to keep on living in radiant spiritual health and growth, our souls must feed on one food only. Don't tamper with the formula. God warns, "Like newborn babies, crave pure spiritual milk [the Bible], so that by it you may grow up in your salvation" (1 Peter

2:2). Third, we must exercise our faith by trusting God to lead. We need to walk in the light obediently the moment God grants the light, and center our lives in Christ. We must get going and keep going! Then his power will keep us from falling. He has all that it takes. The next move is yours. Will you take all that he offers to you now?

**There is a fountain filled with blood,
Drawn from Immanuel's veins;
And sinners plunged beneath that flood
Lose all their guilty stains.**

William Cowper

River of Gold

My father, the late Dr. Lyell Rader, Sr., was raised as a preacher's son in strict Methodism, and learned many Bible verses at the family altar. When he recaptured his boyhood faith, he began to search the Scriptures avidly.

One day he read Exodus 32, the account of how the Hebrews, who God had led out of slavery in Egypt, backslid and worshiped a golden calf. It seemed incredible that people who had seen the awesome power of God overthrow the might of Egypt, who had been so miraculously delivered through the Red Sea and had even heard the voice of God thunder from Sinai like a billion–watt amplifier, could ever again revert to paganism. But as Moses descended from the mountain with the Ten Commandments on the tablets of stone, he saw 3,000 of Israel's men dancing naked around the golden calf in a sexual orgy of idolatry.

Moses smashed the tablets of stone. What was the use of a holy Law for such an unholy people? There was swift and terrible judgment to prevent the cancer from spreading to the whole nation.

Exodus 32:20 reads: "And he took the calf they had made and burned it in the fire; then he ground it to powder, scattered it on the water and made the Israelites drink it." The 30th verse adds, "The next day Moses said to the people, 'You have committed a great sin. But now I will go up to the Lord; perhaps I can make atonement for your sin.'"

My father reflected upon two strongly contradictory words in this verse, "perhaps" and "atonement." Since when, he thought, was there ever a "perhaps" connected with atonement? Every verse he could think of was extremely definite and positive; no ifs or buts.

"Whoever comes to me I will never drive away" are the words of Jesus in John 6:37. Other precious promises came to mind: "If you confess with your mouth, 'Jesus is Lord,' and believe in your heart that God raised him from the dead, you will be saved" (Romans 10:9). Jesus said in Revelation 3:20, "I stand at the door and knock. If anyone hears my voice and opens the door, I will come in and eat with him, and he with me."

Again, "He who has the Son has life; he who does not have the Son of God does not have life" (1 John 5:12). What simple, one–syllable assurances!

There was no double talk about salvation. Then why the word "perhaps"? Oh! he thought. Of course! There was no blood offered, and "without the shedding of blood there is no forgiveness" (Hebrews 9:22). *He could not recall one passage in the Old or New Testament where salvation was ever spoken of without some sort of blood atonement, either literal or figurative.*

There was obviously no blood offered by Moses. But even to dare approach God for forgiveness, there must have been a symbol of blood; hence the perhaps that God might accept the symbol.

My father read again the details of Moses' action in verse 20, searching for the symbolic blood offering. Moses purified the gold by fire, then ground it to powder. Deuteronomy 9:21 adds, "Also I took that sinful thing of yours, the calf you had made, and burned it in the fire. Then I crushed it and ground it to powder as fine as dust and threw the dust into a stream that flowed down the mountain."

My father, a research chemist, recalled that Michael Faraday had made a pink solution by running an electric current through gold wires in water, and called it "colloid of gold." It was not a solution, but particles of gold held in permanent suspension by electrification.

Each charged particle repelled every other particle. He wondered if Moses could have used a better method, and possibly have made a deeper red.

He knew that "Moses was educated in all the wisdom of the Egyptians" as stated in Acts 7:22. He recalled that the sacred scarab beetles, found in many Egyptian tombs, had bright red eyes. Testing a minute speck of the red eye in a spectroscope, the gold line lit up, confirming his guess that Moses had known how to make colloid of gold. Thus my father was determined to trace the steps of the Mosaic process.

He purified some gold using the pure flame of oxygen and hydrogen. He made an emery wheel of magnesite, a common rock found near Sinai, and mounted it on a motor. He placed a beaker of distilled water under the wheel. The moment the gold touched the whirling wheel, the water turned blood–red.

The reason yellow gold can so instantly turn blood–red is because at a critical size (about one millionth of a meter), electrified gold breaks away from the pull of gravity and goes into permanent suspension. This size also happens to be the exact wavelength of red light. Since all colors are in white light, the red ray is strongly reflected to the eye from each particle of gold. He estimated that the stream from Sinai must have run blood–red for several weeks, reminding Israel of the blood–guiltiness of their sin.

Here, then, is the third type of our Savior's blood

recorded in Scripture: animal blood from the animal kingdom, grape juice from the vegetable kingdom and colloid of gold from the mineral kingdom.

Surely, the very rocks cry out the price of our redemption. No more need we grope for a symbol. The Lamb of God has already been offered, "the righteous for the unrighteous, to bring you to God" (1 Peter 3:18). And again, "He himself bore our sins in his body on the tree, so that we might die to sins and live for righteousness; by his wounds you have been healed" (1 Peter 2:24).

He restores harmony between man and his maker,
between man and his brother.

Lyell Rader

IMBALANCE = UNNATURAL

Almost any beginner can raise chickens on a small scale for a few years and get away with it. But if you plan to be in business for more than seven years, you need to know about a strange seven–year cycle, an apparently automatic limiting device to keep nature in balance. It prevents any one crop or creature from taking over the earth by a population explosion.

The mass deaths of the lemming, a mouse–size creature that lives in the Arctic, perfectly illustrates this principle. Overcrowding causes nervous and physical disorders that kill them wholesale, making them panic and rush to their destruction. These disorders also discourage breeding. Whatever the mechanics, just when one more year of astronomical reproduction would be catastrophic, the tidal wave suddenly ceases, and nature is in balance once again.

Think what would happen if every codfish egg laid—5,000,000 at a time—survived and in turn reproduced for six years. The Atlantic Ocean would be packed solid with codfish. And if you think that is bad, seagoing sunfish, weighing tons, lay up to 300,000,000 eggs at a time. Still worse, the spawning sea hare lays 41,000 eggs per minute. At such a rate, if all survived and reproduced for four generations, they would occupy a space six times the volume of the earth!

If one decided to cultivate a weed on a plot of ground for seven years, pests and blight would soon appear from every direction to level off the growth. God is the author of crop rotation. His laws, given to the Israelites, decreed that every seventh year there was to be no plowing or planting. Thus the penalty of pest and blight cycles was avoided.

Left to itself, neither animal nor vegetable kingdoms would get out of balance, but man has a way of transplanting both out of their intended habitats.

Letting the salt water lamprey into the Great Lakes via the St. Lawrence Seaway nearly destroyed a $10,000,000 a year fishing industry. Starlings may not be a problem in their native England, but they are most unwelcome guests here.

American jackrabbits imported to Australia exploded to the point of a national emergency because they had no natural enemies there. In America coyotes keep them under control, but Australian kangaroos don't like to eat them.

Arizona cactus was imported to Australia as cheap fencing. It thrived so well that it took over a land area equal to all of England. Entomologists finally discovered that a little moth kept the cactus under control in Arizona, so the moths were exported to Australia by the billions. The scientists then tried to discover which American birds keep the moths under control.

You can't win when you upset nature. Guesswork and God are two different matters.

Similarly, the human heart tends to trust its own trial-and-error groping, even though God's tried and true methods are free for the taking. *When we fail to allow God to control our lives, they get out of balance.* We're all like loaded dice, inclined to the side of evil. At the root of all problems, personal and communal, is sin. And Christ alone is the answer to that problem.

Not only does Jesus forgive sin, but he balances one's nature. He restores harmony between man and his maker, between man and his brother.

If your life is out of balance, reach for the nail-scarred hand of the one who never betrayed a promise. His invitation, "Come unto me," is open to every man, woman and child. He will revolutionize your life and put it in proper balance.

Where there is true repentance, there is always free forgiveness.

The Salvation Army's
Orders and Regulations for Officers

THE LIGHT THAT CURES & KILLS

X–rays do more than take pictures that penetrate inches of steel. They can also kill cancer cells. In spite of their power, these rays go unnoticed by man. A person could be exposed to a lethal dose of radiation without ever knowing it.

But the common rat can detect x–rays and will manifest great alarm if exposed to even minute amounts of radiation. Without the use of its eyes, a rat can sense the rays even more readily. Even while sleeping, it will awake at the slightest dose and go into a frenzy as it tries to escape, but if radiation is continued for long, the rat will get used to the exposure, relax its panic and eventually go back to sleep and to its death.

In controlled amounts, x–rays can destroy cancer cells, but an overdose can give one cancer.

Years ago, my wife developed a fungal infection on her hands. It was a great embarrassment to her. Her hands would water and scab, then get better, only to go through the same cycle again and again. This continued for seven years. She went to doctor after doctor. Finally we went to a skin specialist.

He frankly admitted that anything persisting for seven years is hard to cure. He then said to my wife, "I want you to recall every x–ray you have ever had. Consult your mother. She may remember some you have forgotten. I intend to give you a massive dose of radiation—so much that you will never again be able to duplicate it. If I fail to give you enough, you will carry this affliction to your grave; if I give you too much it will turn your blood to cancer." Happily his calculation was correct. The cure was complete.

Now, God is faced with the same predicament. He must reveal himself to our eyes of faith just enough to kill the evil cancer of unbelief without killing our capacity to love him. Have you ever wondered why God doesn't come down with overwhelming power and compel the human race to believe him? The right amount of light can cure; too much can kill.

That's why there is no salvation possible for the devil or his angels. They have sinned against all the light there is. The purpose of God's revelation is to lead to repentance. The purpose of his light is to lead to love, or it cannot save. The Lord Jesus took 33½ years to court the human race and woo it from sin to himself. If God's way of the cross doesn't work, nothing will. God deliberately drove Adam and Eve out of the Garden of Eden after they had sinned to shield their rebellious hearts from sinning against more light.

The person I meet in my travels who has the hardest heart is not a prison inmate. I have often led such people to Christ in a single hour. *The person with the hardest heart is one who grew up in a Christian home without becoming a Christian.* Overexposure to light destroys the capacity for sight.

Remember after the rat's first alarm, if radiation is long continued, it gets used to it, relaxes its guard and eventually goes to sleep and to its death. A person can throw off conviction again and again, my friend, but every time he does, he sinks back into a deeper spiritual coma from which he may not awake until it is too late. Far better to feel panic at the thought of defying God—for that's what sin is.

Few people would be willing to commit the unpardonable sin in a single second of blasphemy. But every time a person shrugs God off, he is committing the unpardonable sin on the installment plan. His conscience becomes more calloused. He gets used to living under the wrath of God, until he no longer cares and falls into the sleep of death.

Light is a dangerous thing to fool with. X–ray light can mean life or death to our bodies, but Bible light determines eternal destiny—with God or without him.

John 3:19 says, "This is the verdict: Light has come into the world, but men loved darkness instead of light because their deeds were evil." Jesus declared, "I am the light of the world. Whoever follows me will never walk in darkness, but will have the light of life" (John 8:12).

Not the depth of my sin
But the breadth of his grace,
Not the darkness within
But the light of his face;
Not my weakness of faith
But the surge of his power.
This, this is what counts
As I serve God each hour.

Flora Larsson

POWERING THE
PROJECT

Murray was a young boy whose curiosity was aroused by the tall tales of mysterious goings-on in my "laboratory," up in the third-floor attic. Requesting a conducted tour, Murray got the full treatment, including appropriate shocks on banister and bench, weird hocus-pocus lights emanating from fingers into an old light bulb and sundry other wonders. He left the demonstration burning with ambition.

The next morning he was a total backslider. He thought that electricity was bunk, that Edison was a fake and that I was worse.

"How do you know, Murray?" I asked.

"I tried it," he pouted.

"Pretty big subject to explore all in one night, Murray. What did you try?"

"I electrocuted my wagon! And it won't run!"

Little wonder the electrocuted wagon wouldn't run. He had two dead dry cells with their insides spewing out of their split zinc casings. Had they not been already dead, they soon would have been. They were wired in a way Edison would hardly have recognized (neither in series nor parallel, but drinking each other's juice). To further outrage reason, he had them connected with clothesline instead of wire. One piece was tied to the brake handle, the other to a bolt in the floor, with nary a motor between. And he wondered why his electrocuted wagon wouldn't run!

Backsliders often say, "I tried it and it didn't work." In most cases, backsliding is 90 percent lack of front-sliding. There is a "sloppy easy–going–believism" around that settles for a mental assent instead of real life–transforming "faith, which works by love" (Galatians 5:6). If the love of Christ doesn't draw us to love him back, it isn't saving faith.

The Amplified Bible puts John 1:12 this way: "But to as many as did receive and welcome him, he gave the authority [power, privilege, right] to become the children of God, that is, to those who believe in, adhere to, trust in and rely on, his name." That word "believe" presupposes repentance. Furthermore, it is in a tense we don't possess in English, denoting present, progressive action. You do something about it; you stick and stay stuck; you cleave to him in love; you bet your life on him and go into permanent partnership with him.

Charles Colson tells how the gangster Mickey Cohen once professed conversion. The eager soul winner said, "Mickey, since you are a Christian now, you won't be a gangster any longer."

"Oh, wait a minute," said Mickey, "you have Christian doctors and Christian athletes. Why not Christian gangsters?"

"No, Mickey, you are either a gangster or a Christian. You can't be both."

"Well," said Mickey, "count me out. I can't give up my living." And that was the end of Mickey's profession. He probably still thinks, "I tried it, and it didn't work." Another Murray!

St. Paul thanked God "without ceasing" for the Thessalonian Christians: "Because, when you received the word of God ... you accepted it not as the word of men, but as it actually is, the word of God, which is at work in you who believe" (1 Thessalonians 2:13). This thing works! The Lord Jesus said, "My Father is always at his work to this very day, and I, too, am working" (John 5:17). He never called his deeds miracles, but mighty works.

Our Savior designed salvation to work. Calvary's key exactly fits a sinner's heart. The blood of Christ's cross can save anyone "from the guttermost to the uttermost" who will come to God by him. The most hopeless sinner can become "steadfast, unmovable, always abounding in the work of the Lord" (1 Corinthians 15:58). Salvation will never work on Murray's terms, or on any other person's terms. If it failed, it wasn't God's.

"Whoever comes to me," said Jesus, "I will never drive away" (John 6:37). He not only saves all who come to him, but he can keep them from falling, all the way to Glory (see Jude 20–25). He can power his own project.

If God provides with flawless foresight for every need of every creature, will he forsake the crown of his creation whom he has redeemed at such fearful cost? Never! "And my God will meet all your needs according to his glorious riches in Christ Jesus" (Philippians 4:19).

"For it is by grace you have been saved, through faith—and this not from yourselves, it is the gift of God—not by works, so that no one can boast" (Ephesians 2:8–9). The word "grace" means unmerited favor. However, while we are not saved by good works, take a look at Ephesians 2:10: "For we are God's workmanship, created in Christ Jesus to do good works, which God prepared in advance for us to do."

It is true. We are not saved by good works, but we are saved to do good works. When we are hooked into him, by grace, when all the wires are properly connected to the source, God provides the power.

He left his Father's throne above,
So free, so infinite his grace,
Emptied himself of all but love
And bled for Adam's helpless race.
'Tis mercy all, immense and free,
For, O my God, it found out me.

Charles Wesley

JUNGLE COURTESY

The jungle is governed by the maxim "live and let live." Note the courtesy between trees. If two trees grow up together within three or four feet of one another, they will never fight over which is to grow the most branches between them. They will automatically grow twice as many branches outward as they do in the cramped space between them. If the trees are even closer, as when two or three trees grow out of one root cluster, there will be no significant branches between them—just fuzz. From the air, the two trees appear to be a single tree.

But, if one tree gets a running start and another starts to grow beside it, the first will round out symmetrically. Meanwhile the younger tree will put all of its branches outward—away from its big brother—as if to say, "Alright! You shave at the mirror; I'll scrub my teeth at the tub!"

Even individual leaves display this courtesy and cooperation. You will never find leaves competing for sunshine. They have an amazing sense of one another's presence, and both will move to get out of each other's way so both can drink in their fair share of sunshine.

There are certain parasitic plants that will not germinate, often for years, until a host plant or tree is first growing within easy reach of its tentacles. There are other plants that will not germinate in the presence of certain other seeds, and this antipathy is mutual. They would compete for the same nutrients if they did; therefore, neither would complete its life cycle. So by mutual agreement neither will germinate. However, if you remove either one, the remaining plant will take root and grow.

Seeds of some desert plants lie dormant for years until rain soaks to a depth of six inches. Yet the seeds lie in the top inch of the soil. Who told them that this depth of moisture is necessary if they are to complete their life cycle and seed again? If these plants had sprouted under a single inch of rain, the whole species would have perished.

Why can't people live in harmony the way plants do? Why won't people obey God's laws, the way every other creature does? The answer is sin. *Sin separates brother from brother, husband from wife, mother from daughter, father from son. And sin separates man from God!*

God strikes at the heart of the matter when he cries out in Deuteronomy 5:29: "Oh, that their hearts would be inclined to fear me and keep all my commands always, so that it might go well with them and their children forever!"

The happy news is that God will give such a heart to those who turn to him in repentance and faith. "Therefore, if anyone is in Christ, he is a new creation" (2 Corinthians 5:17). Ask him today for a new heart and discover the joy of living in harmony with God and man. Then you will be able to say with St. Paul, "So I strive always to keep my conscience clear before God and man" (Acts 24:16).

**What God expects us to attempt,
he also enables us to achieve.**

Stephen Olford

WHATEVER GOD
MAKES WORKS

The electric eel of the Amazon River can light up a neon sign, kill a horse at 20 feet and distinguish friend from foe at 40 feet.

The generating mechanism for such voltage is located in three columns running the length of its body. These columns are voltaic piles composed of alternate conductive and dielectric, or insulating, tissue. Each column in a large eel can generate 300 volts at ten amps. These columns are wired in series (negative to positive). Wired in this manner, the combined kick is 900 volts at ten amps, the perfect killing current for fresh water.

The electric ray of the salt water ocean is very different in appearance, but has virtually the same equipment. There are three columns producing 300 volts each at ten amps, but the columns are wired parallel instead of in series (negatives wired together and positives wired together). Wired in this manner, the kick remains at 300 volts, but at three times the current, 30 amps. This is the perfect killing current for salt water.

More questions than answers arise if these ideally adaptive differences in the creatures' wiring are attributed to trial and error or to chaotic chance, rather than the Creator's omniscience.

Another puzzle needing explanation is the switching device for so much current. There are no pitted switch points or burned contacts in either creature. The blast of extremely short duration is electronically triggered by God's own solid state physics.

How long would it take Mother Nature—without design or designer—to accidentally learn the secret of making the hundreds of voltaic piles? What accounts for the serial connections of the one and the parallel wiring of the other? How were these highly specialized creatures given the intricate triggering mechanisms to set off their lethal shocks and the power to distinguish friend from foe? Remember they also have built-in battery chargers. The answer is simple—God.

Granted, some creatures do look unbelievably odd, but they all have one thing in common: they work. This requires four simultaneous endowments: first, complex apparatus; second, instinctive know-how to operate the equipment; third, motivation to operate the equipment at the right moment; and fourth, an environment where it perfectly fits into the balance of nature by just the right ratio of advantage to disadvantage, birthrate to deathrate.

St. Paul wrote, "When you received the word of God, which you heard from us, you accepted it not as the word of men, but as it actually is, the word of God, which is at work in you who believe" (1 Thessalonians 2:13). *Whatever God makes works, and works to perfection. So does his plan for transforming anyone's life from a rat race to a rapture.*

Give him a chance with your life. You can become a new creation in Christ.

Jesus died for our sins so he can blot them out completely. He rose from the dead to empower our present and guarantee an abundant entrance into his glorious everlasting heaven.

Let the beauty of Jesus be seen in me,
All his wonderful passion and purity,
O, thou Spirit divine, all my nature refine,
Till the beauty of Jesus be seen in me.

Song Book of The Salvation Army

FOR GLORY &
FOR BEAUTY

This is an age of color. You see splotches and splashes of it everywhere—psychedelic, flores-cent, phosphorescent and iridescent. Yet none of these can beat the glory of a sunset or the beauty of the lilies. Jesus said, "I tell you that not even Solomon in all his splendor was dressed like one of these" (Matthew 6:29).

Colors are produced in many ways, such as with dyes and pigments. Prisms also produce colors by breaking white light into its sevenfold spectrum. A drop of oil on water, as it spreads across the surface, suddenly becomes red; then parts of it swirl thinner and it becomes orange; still thinner and it becomes yellow, green, blue, indigo and violet, as it passes through the various thicknesses, or should we say, thinnesses, of the wavelengths of these colors.

The beautiful blue morpho butterfly of the tropics owes its iridescent wings to thousands of colorless water–clear platelets hewn to the wavelength of the blue ray. It is the secret of every iridescent feather, whether it be the throat of a hummingbird or the great seven–foot tail feather of a prize peacock. The very parts of a feather are interesting: first the quill, then the barbs. Out of the barbs come the barbules and from them spring the barbicels and, finally, the hooklets which zip up a living feather. This explains how a parakeet can mess up its feathers in a bath, then with a single shiver, step out of its beauty parlor with every hair back in place. There are billions of these zippers on every bird, so no curlers are ever needed.

The green parakeet does not really have green feathers. There is a transparent yellow stain in the barbs, but the barbicels are the exact thickness to throw a blue iridescence over the yellow feather, which makes it green. One can breed out the blue and get a yellow parakeet, or breed out the yellow and get a blue parakeet, or breed out both and get a white, but that's the limit. Varieties are never infinite. They are built–in potentials, part of the divine purpose.

The peacock's glory is not finished with a mere splash of colors. There is only one eye to a feather. Every feather is precisely the right length and held in the right position so as to produce a perfect geometrical design, called an exploding pantograph.

Every year all the feathers must fall out, so an extra row of eyes can be added to the new plumage the next spring. If one feather refuses to fall out, the pattern is destroyed next season, for all the eyes of that row have moved out and left the old feather behind, spoiling the perfect pattern.

It seems that God went to a lot of trouble to make some things for glory and for beauty (see Exodus 28:2). If there is but little beauty in your life and much monotony and dullness, "Let the beauty of the Lord our God be upon you" (Psalm 90:17).

The Holy Spirit, dwelling within, turns our eyes from that which is temporal to that which is eternal; from the trial itself to God's purposes in the trial.

Commissioner Samuel Logan Brengle

SYMBIOTIC PARTNERSHIP

The strangest creatures team up in symbiotic partnership. For instance a little bird is allowed to pick the teeth of a crocodile. Actually the bird goes after leeches that hurt the croc's gums.

A moth that never saw its mother hunts for a flower it has never seen. Its body is the exact length necessary to lay its eggs in the bloom. When baby wakes up as a little, flat worm with a ravenous appetite, it finds the perfect balanced diet in a succulent layer between the seed and the shell, but it has to work for it.

If it does a good job of switching and snapping and tumbling about to get each successive mouthful, it jounces and bounces the seed around, as much as one hundred feet, until it finds a moist crevice of earth. The seed germinates and splits open the capsule that could have been a coffin, liberating the little worm to pupate and become another moth to repeat the cycle. The new seed grows to become another Mexican jumping bean.

Smyrna figs are indebted to a tiny fig wasp. The wasp is born on the fig trees, feeds on the trees and fertilizes the trees. The yucca plant is dependent on a tiny, white moth. Much of the vegetable kingdom is indebted to the lowly honeybee.

The great rhinoceros has its tick birds, and wing-weary ruby throated humming birds are quick to hitch a ride on the tails of a flock of Canadian geese during migration.

The vegetable kingdom perfectly complements the animal kingdom. The first breathes in carbon dioxide and breathes out oxygen. The second breathes in oxygen and breathes out carbon dioxide. Our ecology would really be in trouble if both competed for oxygen or if carnivorous animals were as prolific as herbivorous animals. If skunks were as prolific as rabbits, there wouldn't be enough chlorophyll in the woods to decontaminate the atmosphere.

The world of nature is a vast single plan, each facet interdependent with others and the whole intricately and exquisitely balanced and counterbalanced. Psalm 19:1 says, "The heavens declare the glory of God; the skies proclaim the work of his hands." The more we learn, the more we stand in awe of the Creator, who seems to delight in infinite variety, beauty and order.

But the most amazing partnership of all is the Lord Jesus becoming man in order to reconcile the rebel human race with the holy God of all power. In one stroke, Calvary love forgives our sins, captures our hearts and changes our natures. By his atonement, Christ welds our helplessness to his omnipotence for the single purpose of doing his will, and we share his purpose of redeeming lost humanity. "Oh, the depth of the riches of the wisdom and knowledge of God! How unsearchable his judgments, and his paths beyond tracing out!" (Romans 11:33).

God has put his heart on paper.

Frederick Booth–Tucker

THE MARVELOUS TONGUE

ongues are remarkable organs and unbelievably varied. The tongue of some hummingbirds is a slender paintbrush; the fuzz on the tip holds a drop of nectar. Other hummingbirds depend upon their bills closing so tightly on the sides that their tongues can be used as a straw, but this only works because their bills are flared open at the tip.

The tongue of a frog can shoot out like a bullet. The tip has an adhesive substance like sticky flypaper. Its tongue is exactly long enough for the amphibian to creep within range of its insect prey without warning it.

The African chameleon has a similar tongue that can shoot out beyond the length of its body—nearly 18 inches. The mechanics of such marksmanship are unique. The hollow tongue is threaded back upon a slippery, tapered bone in the throat. A circle of muscle surrounding this combination has the power of explosive contraction. A chameleon rarely misses any butterfly on the wing that gets within its 18–inch range.

The tongue of the African anteater is long and thin enough to worm its way down an anthill. Its unusual saliva is not an ordinary adhesive. It has no attraction for dirt or sand, yet it sticks tight to the eggs and bodies of ants unlucky enough to be caught in its path.

Woodpeckers have tongues with other properties. The yellowhammer or flicker has a tongue with a needle–sharp point and six barbs. It needs the sharp point to pierce the armored body of a tree grub, and it needs the barbs to hold it while it pulls the grub back into its mouth. It also needs several inches of length in order to reach the tree grub.

A limp tongue, like that of the frog or chameleon, would not do. This tongue must have the capability of turning a 90 degree angle, yet remain stiff as an arrow shaft as it flashes right and left into the bore of the insect. The yellowhammer's tongue can extend four inches beyond its bill. Nothing shorter would do if grubs are to be its diet. God knew how to design the right creature with the right equipment and the right instinct to do the job to keep nature in balance.

God gave man a tongue which, above all, is an organ

of speech. Unlike the lower creation, which can only utter fixed songs or signals, man can speak at will. He may choose to use his tongue for blessing or for cursing. The Lord Jesus warned: "For by your words you will be acquitted, and by your words you will be condemned" (Matthew 12:37).

God also communicates with man in words. Jesus said, "I tell you the truth, whoever hears my word and believes him who sent me has eternal life and will not be condemned; he has crossed over from death to life" (John 5:24).

Whether God thundered his word from the summit of Sinai, or crystallized his word in print in the Bible, or came in person as the Living Word to fulfill each prophecy concerning himself, it is all equally authoritative. And it is a matter of eternal life or eternal doom whether we accept or reject that word. It is our only life preserver.

You have everything to gain if that word is true. No hope is to be found in any other direction. So hear, repent, believe, and be born again. Then use your tongue to tell others of his great salvation.

**The will of God will not take you
where the grace of God cannot keep you.**

Anonymous

You Can't
Surprise God

While human mothers ordinarily outweigh their offspring by an average of 20 to 22 times, the great kodiak mother bear outweighs her newborn cub by as much as 880 times. The kodiak cub is born in the midst of hibernation. Mother wakes up just long enough to cradle baby at her bosom; then both go back to sleep. In the spring, mother bear wakes up rather gaunt, but baby bear has become a bouncing toddler, having gained several pounds from its birth weight of a few ounces.

But this is nothing compared with the great gray kangaroo. Mama kangaroo outweighs her offspring by as much as 3,000 times. The tiny creature looks more like an insect than a mammal when it is born. Several of them could be held in a teaspoon.

The ungainly little creature is coaxed up mother's abdomen as she licks a path into her pouch. There the baby kangaroo soon finds one of the milk stations. Strangely, however, the baby has no sucking muscles. It knows where to put the nipple, but it can't do anything with it. Mother comes to the rescue and expels the milk, but if the baby happened to be on "channel A" and mother accidentally started pumping "channel B," she could drown the baby. So the wise Creator gave her "stereo control."

However, almost all living creatures cannot drink and breathe at the same time. A flip–flop trap door floors over the breathing tube or windpipe while swallowing and vice versa. Therefore, no one can drink at the timing of another's will.

There are two notable exceptions to this usual ingenious arrangement. Serpents, which swallow their prey whole and often take several hours to get it down, would die without being able to breathe. So God has given them an extra extension to their windpipe. They hang it out of the side of their mouths like a snorkel so they can breathe no matter how long it takes to swallow their prey.

The other exception to the flip–flop valve is the baby kangaroo. It too has a snorkel extension to its windpipe, but, instead of being located in the mouth like the snake's, it is tucked behind its uvula into its nostril. Thus the baby kangaroo can breathe while it is nursing—even at mother's timing.

Absolutely nothing catches God by surprise. He foresees every emergency and makes ample provision for every need. His commands are really promises, because what he commands, he gives the ability to do.

When Jesus looked at the paralyzed man at the Pool of Bethesda and knew that he had been in this helpless condition for 38 years, our Lord gave him three seemingly impossible commands. The poor fellow couldn't obey the first one, much less all three.

But look who issued the command to "Get up! Pick up your mat and walk" (John 5:8). The God of all Creation was speaking. So the paralyzed man rose, took up his bed and walked. This is par for the course. God never gives a command without giving instant, enabling grace.

This same God has commanded, "Repent, then, and turn to God, so that your sins may be wiped out, that times of refreshing may come from the Lord" (Acts 3:19). Turn to him now and seek salvation from the penalty and power of sin.

We don't have to be afraid if our wills are weak, "for it is God who works in you to will and to act according to his good purpose" (Philippians 2:13). He will help us with both the willing and the doing. Another precious promise we can bet our lives on is Hebrews 12:2: "Let us fix our eyes on Jesus, the author and perfecter of our faith, who for the joy set before him endured the cross, scorning its shame, and sat down at the right hand of the throne of God."

Some say, "I don't want to start something I can't finish." Well, the good news is that God started this fabulous plan of salvation, and he has vowed to finish it for every sinner who sincerely wants to be reconciled with his maker.

He will also release us from evil habits. First Corinthians 10:13 tells us, "No temptation has seized you except what is common to man. And God is faithful; he will not let you be tempted beyond what you can bear. But when you are tempted, he will also provide a way out so that you can stand up under it."

Every invention of man starts out as a clumsy prototype. It often takes years to get out all the bugs. But there are no bugs in God's creation. Even the crawling and flying kinds function at peak efficiency. They don't need improvement, because they fit perfectly into the balance of nature.

God knows what we can bear. God knows what we need. He knows our make–up because he made us. What he made us to do, he will enable us to do.

PART II:

HINTS OF THE
HOLY LIFE

O make my hand a hand
Of faith, my eye faith's eye,
My feet to march in faith along
Where Jesus' standards fly,
My ear, O Christ, to hear
Above the noise, for me
Thine unseen trumpets sounding clear
The song of victory.

Commissioner Edward Read

THE SOUND
BARRIER

hen a terrible explosion occurred during World War II in Perth Amboy, New Jersey, everybody feared the Nazis had invaded the country. Telephone lines were jammed, but soon the radio calmed our fears. It was only a sonic explosion, the announcer explained; a new plane had pierced the sound barrier.

Previously, pilots had reported that they couldn't push their planes past 741.1 miles per hour, even when they gunned their engines. There was something up there that held them back. Many doubted the validity of the pilots' claims, but finally a scientist went up and provided verification.

A search was begun for other things that might also travel 741.1 miles per hour. It was discovered that sound traveled at that speed, roughly 1,000 feet per second. Evidently, the invisible molecules of air dawdled around at that speed and piled up like an invisible snow bank in front of the plane, resisting any increase in speed beyond 741.1.

Two important modifications were made to the plane: the addition of a needle nose that could pierce the bank of air, and the removal of unnecessary fat on the fuselage to conform to the shape of the slipstream upon passing through this invisible snow bank. If you multiply the huge number of square inches on the surface of a plane by 15 pounds of atmospheric pressure per square inch at sea level, you will find that tons of pressure have been pried apart.

When this happens and the split air comes banging back together, you have a sonic boom. It's the same reason lightning causes thunder. The lightning rips the air apart and the air comes banging together again in a clap of thunder.

Similarly, Christians can run into a spiritual sound barrier. After they have grown in grace for a time, they generally find they do not seem to be able to progress any further.

Why is this? Interference.

Satan doesn't care how many feeble Christians there are, but he strongly resists anyone aspiring to follow

Paul's command to "stand firm. Let nothing move you. Always give yourselves fully to the work of the Lord" (1 Corinthians 15:58). He will try anything and everything to distract us from the pursuit of holiness.

However, we don't need to wallow around in the seventh chapter of Romans—the old "wretched man that I am" syndrome—because God has provided that we can and should be "more than conquerors through him that loved us" (Romans 8:37). We can have victory on every front.

If your children are young, it might be good to give them alternative words for holiness, a term that sounds impossible to a child. The Amplified Bible uses "unbroken fellowship" in its translation of Romans 6:11. The Keswick Convention has the theme "the victorious life." The Canadian Prairie Bible Institute speaks of "the crucified life." Another Bible conference defines it as "the abundant life."

But "holiness" is a good Bible word if you take time to explain it. It's not absolute perfection of performance. It is purity of the heart, purity of intention.

If we wholeheartedly love God, and want to please him, that is all he requires. If we are wholly his, he counts it as holy.

You might think, "How can a human be holy like God?" Alone he can't, but when the Holy Ghost indwells a sinner, he can be like God, since the Spirit does the living. He is the Holy One; we just invite him to be our Lord. The best we can do is present our bodies "as living sacrifices," wholly. If he wants to spell our wholly with an h, that's his business.

It helps to consider the alternatives. For example, how about halfliness or three–quarterliness, or even nine–tenthliness? That was the sin of Israel. Consider Solomon, who "showed his love for the Lord by walking according to the statutes of his father David, except that he offered sacrifices and burned incense on the high places" to please his ungodly wives (1 Kings 3:3).

Purity and holiness are expected and required in many areas of life. Doctors demand pure medicines, including pure water. They would never think of using tap water for medicines. They use distilled water.

Banks want accountability to the last penny. Athletes give themselves totally to "going for the gold." And top concert pianists spend hours at the keyboard daily.

In marriage, a wife expects 100 percent faithfulness from her husband, and vice versa. Forsaking all others, "being faithful to her as long as you both shall live," is the marriage vow. Why should we expect God to settle for anything less from us?

Now to obtain this unbroken fellowship with God, we need a crucifixion of our will. We must abdicate the throne of our life to the King of kings. We must give up our ways for his ways. We must count ourselves "dead to sin but alive to God in Christ Jesus" (Romans 6:11).

By the time our children were in eighth grade, my wife

and I urged them to give God half an hour, and to put it ahead of everything else, including homework, television or play. If we don't make God's time first, we will never find time. Satan will see to it that we just don't get around to it.

We didn't have them get up in the morning; we had them get down. They rolled out of bed onto their knees and looked into Jesus' face before they looked into anybody else's face.

Then we had a memory verse at breakfast and a football huddle at the door with a kiss, a prayer and a promise. Then we sent them to school with Bibles under their arms.

Carrying their Bibles to school opened up opportunities for witness, or thrust it upon them, especially when it had a scarlet jacket emblazoned with "Holy Bible" in large letters.

The children spent five or ten minutes in their study hour reading their Bible. When they got home, their mother would remind them to finish their time with God before they did anything else.

Yes, there is an invisible devil who will oppose us the moment we try to do the will of God. We must expect a fight, for it will surely come, but the battle is not ours, it is the Lord's.

When we come out victorious, we will have done three things, described in Jude 1:20–25. First, we will spend time with God daily by digging into his word.

Second, prayer will be our delight. Third, we will receive a baptism of love for God, for his word, for Jesus himself and for others.

Then, according to Jude 1:24, we can expect God to do three things for us that are totally beyond our strength, but well within his power. First, he is able to keep us from falling. Second, he is able to present us faultless before the presence of his glory. Third, he'll give us heaven right here on earth. The Amplified New Testament renders it, "unspeakable ecstatic delight in triumphant joy and exultation" (Jude 1:25).

Go over this again and see if it isn't what you want. It pierces the sound barrier; you die to self and live unto God in partnership with him and his sanctifying power. All you want is the will of your glorious God.

When we mind our three conditions, his are automatic. This was all paid for at Calvary.

Finally, what about that "needle nose" or single purpose? How about getting rid of all excess baggage? As Hebrews 12:1 urges us, "let us throw off everything that hinders and the sin that so easily entangles." For instance, there's nothing wrong with a little TV, but when it robs us of time with God, it's gone too far. It becomes an idol, and God will never play second fiddle to an idol. We only get baptized with fire when we want God more than anything else.

Do you know what you have to do to backslide?
Absolutely nothing.

J. Donald Freese

Evaporation &
Refrigeration

My neighbor once told me he was planning to cut down a big buckeye tree in front of his bedroom; he said he needed to remove it to get more ventilation. I told him he'd be cutting down about $10,000 worth of free air-conditioning, since anything that evaporates, refrigerates.

It is estimated that a tree six inches in diameter will evaporate half a ton of water into the air in 24 hours. That makes a six-inch tree a half-ton air conditioner. Imagine how much water an Ohio buckeye tree twice the height of a house would evaporate!

I used a spray can of component refrigerant to show him what I meant. This liquid becomes a gas almost instantly when it is sprayed, so it becomes very cold. I sprayed the refrigerant on a dial thermometer's little bi–metal coil, the part that moves the dial. It dropped the temperature from 70 degrees Fahrenheit to 20 or 30 degrees below zero in one or two seconds. My neighbor didn't cut down the tree.

Anything that evaporates, refrigerates. That's why it is so much cooler in the shade. For example, a black car sitting under bright sunlight on a hot day will get so hot inside you could almost fry an egg on the front seat. But if you walk out of the bright sunlight into a grove of trees, what a relief! Those trees have cooled all out of doors 15 degrees. So if it were 90 degrees outside in the sun, it would be a very comfortable 75 degrees in the shade of those trees.

We've already talked about the three things babies need to do to stay alive and grow (breathe, eat and exercise) and how these, for the Christian, can be compared to prayer, Bible study and obedience.

It's impossible to exercise when we don't feel well. If we stop breathing, we become unconscious and eventually die. If we stop eating, we become weaker and weaker and do not feel like exercising. So the first two are causes, and not exercising is a result.

What does this have to do with it being cooler in the shade? Anything that evaporates, refrigerates. *So, if prayer time and Bible study evaporate, love for Jesus and the motivation to please and obey him refrigerate.*

It's not a matter of trying harder to obey and working on willpower. Rather, what we need is to reestablish our prayer life and Bible study. Then willpower will take care of itself. We will delight in being in the secret of his presence and hiding in his power.

Let's not cut down that tree! Let's not cut out our prayer time or our Bible study time. Instead, let's hide his precious promises in our hearts and minds. For if we do these things, "we will never fall" (2 Peter 1:10).

The all–wise Creator never starts something he cannot finish. This is true of people as well as of plants. When Christ saves a person, he fully provides for the complete life cycle.

Anonymous

GROWTH & DEATH

I srael was commanded to conquer the Promised Land. God said, "I will send an angel before you and drive out the Canaanites, Amorites, Hittites, Perizzites, Hivites and Jebusites" (Exodus 33:2).

This appears to be rough treatment, but it was a perfect parallel of what God himself did in Heaven. He had to throw out every rebellious angel—one third of his heavenly host! Even his archangel, Lucifer, a name that means "son of the morning," had turned into the devil and had to be cast out.

Heaven had to be a clean place for clean beings, or it would quickly become a hell of wickedness.

When I was a boy, I attempted to grow corn in an

inch or two of soil on top of ledge rock. My plow kept rolling over on its edge, scraping the rock as it ran into the abutments of each ledge, breaking the wooden plugs that connected the plows to my tractor. I got tired of backing up and replacing the wooden plugs, so I decided to put in an iron bolt. When I hit the next ledge, the bolt didn't break. Instead, the tractor reared up and nearly fell over on me before I could hit the clutch and get it out of gear.

An old farmer warned me I couldn't grow corn there. I asked "Why not?"

"Why, you don't have any depth of earth," came the answer. "Corn has got to go down."

But I insisted, "I'm going to plant wider rows so the roots can grow out sideways if they can't grow down."

"You can't tell corn which way to grow. It wants to grow down!"

I stubbornly finished my plowing and planted the corn on the rock. Although I had also planted corn two weeks earlier on a distant hillside, the first corn up was in my rocky soil. But by mid–July, the rocky soil's water had evaporated and its little green flags of victory had drooped, turned brown and died. I pulled some up out of the parched, cracked earth. Their pitiful little roots were like birds' claws blunted from trying to get through the rock.

Farmers understand the parable of the sower in Luke 8:5–15. They know that the seed scattered by the sower on the wayside or roadway never had a chance. The birds got it before daybreak. They also know that, though the seed sowed in rocky soil would have sprouted for a while, it too had no chance. It is just as impossible to build faith on a rock–hard, impenitent heart. The seed must have adequate depth. We've got to break up the fallow ground. The good ground is deep soil where the taproot can go down, grip the earth and reach out for water before the plant ever shows above the turf.

Good ground must also be thoroughly and constantly cultivated. The corn that is crowded with weeds and thorns may live, but will never produce full ears of corn. The knives of the cultivator must rip out all the weeds every few days and pile the earth up against the stalks. Weeds have a way of growing faster than the corn. If they ever get the jump on the farmer, he won't know the difference between weeds and corn. He will pull up corn with the weeds.

So too a fruit–bearing Christian must be a deeply rooted and actively cultivated Christian. We only hurt people by making them rocky–soil Christians. The first squabble is usually enough to cause them to backslide totally. In the words of Charles G. Finney, "The only provision God ever made for the prevention of backsliding is holiness." We must get those weeds out all at once, and keep them out with daily cultivation.

It's like getting rid of cockroaches. Destroy the last

pregnant female or you are soon back to square one again. That's why traps alone are not the answer. Only poison that they bring back to the nest will destroy them completely.

That's why we need to be "dead to sin but alive to God in Christ Jesus" (Romans 6:11). As Jesus "died to sin once for all," we are to be done with sin once and for all (Romans 6:10). And if we have any concept of the awful cost of our salvation, we will hate the old sin life that crucified him and want to spend eternity with such a Savior.

To walk with God, we must run to God.

George Gritter

POWER STEERING

W hat a blessing it is to have power steering, especially if a medical ailment or simple old age makes even routine motions difficult. While power steering makes it easy to turn and park, drivers still have to exert a little force. If they don't start the action, the invisible giant under the hood will not fur nish his. It's a partnership of power.

God also intends us to be partners with him. There is a vast difference, though, between working for God and "working together with God." It's a tragedy to be busy in one corner doing something for God, when God wants us in another place working together with him.

When we decide what we will do for God, we are in charge. After we make him Lord of all, he is in charge, and we pray with St. Paul, "Lord, what wilt thou have me to do?" (Acts 9:6, KJV).

God will not work through a man who thinks he knows it all and wants to call the shots. Faith always involves obedience or it is not biblical faith. It also presupposes repentance. When saving faith dawns, one has already turned from the darkness toward the light. Then faith moves in and delivers "from the power of Satan to God, so that they may receive forgiveness of sins and a place among those who are sanctified by faith in me" (Acts 26:18). These are the words of Jesus to St. Paul as he stopped him on the Damascus Road.

I can see no real reason why there is usually some delay between salvation and God's full inheritance of sanctification, except our ignorance of what is promised. We can't very well ask for a blessing when we're ignorant of what God is willing to give. Generally, there is a period of growth in grace and acquaintance with God's promises before we dare to ask God for complete victory on every front.

Now there are rare exceptions, like St. Paul, who was well versed in the Scriptures to begin with. He only needed to know that Jesus was the promised Messiah. He already knew that God commanded holiness.

Madame Sheik, a Muslim noblewoman, in her book, *I Dared to Call Him Father*, describes a vision of Jesus with his arms outstretched, welcoming her. Instinctively, she knew it was Jesus. She sent her servant out to find a Christian Bible. When she came to the New Testament, she saw in John 3:3 and 16–21 that she must be born again. So she simply prayed for new birth, and she received that sweet, blessed assurance of his Spirit witnessing with her spirit that she was now his born–again child.

When she read that believers were baptized, she baptized herself in the tub, and when she learned that she must be filled with the Holy Spirit, she prayed for and received sanctification.

After her conversion, she had to flee for her life or her father would have killed her for turning away from Islam. When Madame Sheik arrived in the United States, she sought out evangelist Catherine Kuhlman, whose radio broadcasts she had heard. Ms. Kuhlman interviewed her over the air and marveled at Sheik's spiritual maturity. Her only teacher had been the Spirit through the word.

Similarly, when Major Rusty Tomlinson, a missionary officer, first came to The Salvation Army, she was an unbeliever, but the first time she heard a salvation message, she was saved. The first time she heard of sanctification, she was sanctified. The first time she heard we enrolled soldiers, she requested enrollment. The first time she heard of Officers' Training College, she applied. And the first time she heard we had foreign missions, she offered herself for missionary service. There are not many Rusty Tomlinsons or Madame

Sheiks. Sanctification is a second blessing for most.

St. Paul also had power steering: "To this end I labor, struggling with all his energy, which so powerfully works in me" (Colossians 1:29). We can have it too. And what a wonderful difference between conventional steering, where you do it all, and power steering, where your feeble efforts are greatly amplified.

Power brakes are another boon. Not only are the steps of a good man ordered of the Lord, but so, also, are his stops, according to Psalm 37:23. While my son, Lt. Colonel Damon Rader, was in Africa as a young officer, he once surveyed a creek bed for a possible dam. The grass was high and he was walking at a good pace when suddenly he felt an urge to stop. As he did, a cobra slithered across his path. It would have nailed him if he had not stopped. The stops of a good man are ordered of the Lord, as well as his steps.

Remember that we can neither steer nor stop if the engine stalls. For without a running engine we can do nothing. And Jesus warned in John 15:5, "apart from me you can do nothing."

Conversion does not make a man different from what God made him; it can only make him what God intended him to be, and that is different from what he has made of himself.

George B. Smith

POWER STEERING
IN
FLESH & BLOOD

---

he Asbury Park, New Jersey corps often conducted its salvation meeting in the band shell
above the boardwalk. The meeting consisted of a
sacred concert followed by testimonies and a soul-
winning message.

Once during the prayer meeting that followed the
service, a big fellow and his wife came to the front to
receive the Lord. I visited them early the next morning.
For over a week I saw them every day, and after that
about three or four times a week for a long time.
Another officer, Colonel Frank Guldenschuh, also took
a great interest in them, visiting five or six days a week.

The converts were Edward Gleason, a cousin of
comedian Jackie Gleason, and his wife Shirley. Ed came

from a wonderful family. He and Jackie were raised as brothers. Ed grew up in church and Sunday school and never touched a drop of liquor until the night of the high school prom.

In less than a year, Ed became a hopeless alcoholic, and for 40 years was a derelict. Clever, with the gift of gab, he could talk his way into any number of jobs, but would quickly drink his way out of them. For those 40 years, he lived by his wits from one skid row to another. In fact, he and Shirley had just come out of a bar the night they were converted.

For ten years, Colonel Guldenschuh and I nurtured Ed in the Lord. Once we almost lost him. He and another Salvationist got to squabbling over (believe it or not) who should lead the prayer meeting. I rushed to him and reminded him that obedience to Christ meant forgiving to be forgiven. We went carefully over portions of the Sermon on the Mount (Matthew 5:9–12, 23–24 and 43–45) and also Mark 11:23–26.

During this period Ed's diabetes kicked up, and he had one leg amputated, but the stump would not heal for many, many weeks. One day he saw his adversary coming out of the corps building toward him. The two men fell into one another's arms and were reconciled. Only then did the stump heal.

Soon the other leg became ulcerated, and surgery was scheduled. The night before the surgery was to be performed, we offered united prayer for Ed. In the small hours of the following morning, Ed noticed his foot wasn't hurting. He reached down to touch it and didn't feel any pain. He swung his foot out of bed and thumped it on the floor, then yelled his head off for joy. Several nurses came running in, thinking, based on the amount and volume of noise he was making, that he was in great distress, but they were soon celebrating this miracle with him.

Eventually, the surgeon came to prepare him mentally for the surgery.

Ed said, "There isn't going to be any surgery."

"Oh, yes there is. Unless you want to let that rotting leg kill you."

Ed said, "Look at it." The doctor pulled the leg up, bent over it, then blurted out, "It doesn't stink any more." It was not only clean and odorless, but healed. No surgery was performed on Ed the next day.

One would think that losing a leg would have taught him a lesson about forgiving to be forgiven, but before long Ed, now walking around on an artificial leg, developed an unforgiving attitude once again.

I said, "Ed, after all God has done for you, aren't you ashamed to be so unforgiving of your own brother?"

"Oh, I forgive him," he growled, "but keep him out of my sight. I get a bellyache every time I look at him."

I told him, "God doesn't say, 'Growl out an apology.' He says, 'Be reconciled to your brother.'"

But not until Ed lost the other leg did he awaken to

the fact that saving faith and healing faith mean obedient faith that works by love (see Acts 6:7; Romans 15:18; 2 Corinthians 2:9; Romans 6:17; and Hebrews 11:8). Gradually, Ed became mature spiritually and gave a powerful witness. He was reconciled with his brother Stanley, who took him back to Scranton, Ohio to live in a lovely high–rise apartment.

If any man ever came out of a garbage dump to become "a royal diadem in the hands of his God," Ed, who is now in Glory, was that man (Isaiah 62:3). He, like us, would never have made it on his own strength. Romans 9:16 states, "It does not, therefore, depend on man's desire or effort, but on God's mercy." *So will-power isn't the secret, and neither is muscle power, but simple faith in God's power.*

This is power steering indeed: our feeble faith coupled with God's omnipotence.

Come, Holy Ghost, thy mighty aid bestowing!
Destroy the works of sin, the self, the pride;
Burn, burn in me, my idols overthrowing;
Prepare my heart for him, for my Lord crucified.

Catherine Booth–Clibborn

BAPTIZED
WITH FIRE

When a pilot trains for blind flying, he has to ignore the scene ahead of him and glue his eyes on his instrument panel.

I talked once with a pilot who had flown 100 missions over "the Hump," as they called the Himalayas, during World War II. Only once could he see where he was going, and it nearly scared him to death. He flew up the fog–laden canyons in the dead of night to avoid radar detection, and had to trust his instruments. Even when the clouds lifted and he was in daylight, he dared not trust his eyes, for little puffs of cloud still could obscure towering peaks only discernible by radar.

While training for blind flying in those days, the pilot wore a long, peaked cap that blocked his vision out of the window, but revealed his instrument panel. If he got panicky, he could flip the peak back and see out of the window.

God is training us in much the same way. He promised childless Abraham that his seed would be as numberless as the sands of the sea or the stars of Heaven. Then God waited until Abraham was 100 years old before giving him Isaac.

God often uses the element of waiting to cultivate our patience. God's delays are not denials. Sometimes when we pray for healing, there is a frustrating delay, and the symptoms loom large on the horizon so that our "faith—of greater worth than gold, which perishes even though refined by fire—may be proved genuine and may result in praise, glory and honor when Jesus Christ is revealed" (1 Peter 1:7). Note that this long sentence (1 Peter 1:6–9), while starting with reference to trials in verse 6, ends in verse 9 with inexpressible and glorious joy and our resurrected bodies in Glory.

God knows what he's doing when he stretches our faith. The violin can't make music until the strings are stretched. Muscles can't grow until they are strained. Athletes have a saying, "No pain—no gain."

How deep is our belief? We claim to believe God for the eternal future safety of our souls, but hesitate on the brink of trusting him for the here and now. That's not much faith.

God is training us for leadership in his eternal glory.

Look at Revelation 3:21: "To him who overcomes, I will give the right to sit with me on my throne, just as I overcame and sat down with my Father on his throne." This is no small issue. It is no wonder that the Amplified Bible renders 1 Peter 1:7, "So that the genuineness of your faith may be tested, which is infinitely more precious than the perishable gold which is tested and purified by fire."

We need the fire. *We need the baptism of fire to purge these hearts so prone to doubting.* God didn't save Isaac from the poised knife until the last moment, when the angel caught the plunging arm, for Abraham "did not waver through unbelief regarding the promise of God, but was strengthened in his faith and gave glory to God, being fully persuaded that God had power to do what he had promised" (Romans 4:20–21). Thank God for the purging, purifying, empowering fire.

John the Baptist said, "I baptize you with water for repentance. But after me will come one who is more powerful than I, whose sandals I am not fit to carry. He will baptize you with the Holy Spirit and with fire" (Matthew 3:11).

Gold and silver are refined and purified by fire. Fire only destroys the dross, which is worthless.

Fire also destroys germs. When London was stricken with the black plague, people were dying by the thousands. It took the Great Fire to rid the city of its vermin and purge away the plague. Fire purifies. We need not be afraid of it. God wants our hearts pure, and what he commands, he enables us to do. We need to pray until the fire falls.

"Our God is a consuming fire" (Hebrews 12:29). We need our old Adam nature destroyed so that we might be alive to God. Fire: what a symbol of the Holy Spirit—baptizing, destroying the works of the devil, purifying and empowering!

Our sacrifice must go up in flames. The lordship of our own lives must be handed over to the King of kings and the Lord of lords. This is usually a painful process. Few people die easily to self and to sin, but there is no other path to power with God. We must abdicate the throne of our will and replace it with his will.

When everything is on the altar, God's baptizing fire surely falls, and we surely know it. Oh, the preciousness of Jesus from that moment on!

**It is ordained in the eternal constitution of things
that men of intemperate minds cannot be free.
Their passions forge their fetters.**

Edmund Burke

WHAT PRICE LIBERTY?

$\mathbb{P}$atrick Henry was willing to pay dearly for his creed: "Give me liberty or give me death." A softer generation might prefer the philosophy of the song "Don't Fence Me In." But is fenceless liberty possible, or is it a contradiction in terms?

During a flight from New York City to Alabama in 1957, I saw well–fenced liberty. Watching the smoothly spinning blades of a Viscount, I tried to conceive of the prodigious power behind one propeller as it cut a 14–foot swath through the air at better than 300 miles an hour.

Then it occurred to me that the real hero of the drama was not just the turbo engine, but the mighty ball–bearings that move within prescribed limits to transmit every ounce of energy in the desired direction. Had the ball–bearings been even slightly loose, vibration would have torn off the wing. Had they been too tight, friction would have caused the wing to burst into flame. Perfection was expected and achieved in those bearings because nothing less would do.

If a boy's kite could talk, it might argue with its little master on the ground, slowly paying out the string: "Let me loose! I want to fly! You're holding me down!" True, if the boy were to cut the string, the kite might surge upward for a moment, but then it would soon plunge downward, for the thing that keeps it up is the thing that holds it down. In humans, as in the kite, liberty is achieved by law.

James 1:25 makes it abundantly evident that "the perfect law that gives freedom" and doing the will of God are synonymous terms. Verse 26 of the same chapter even speaks of a rein, and verse 27 shows that this is voluntarily imposed. Earlier in this chapter, all temptation is revealed to be any deviation from God's good and perfect gifts. Temptation ends in death. Some would like to make the terms easy, even sloppy, but God's norm is as invariable as light and allows no tampering with the terms.

The first question a godly wife asked her husband, a preacher, upon his return from leading a meeting was, "Did you have liberty?" She was really asking if he had been totally under the control of the Holy Spirit.

Power without control is unthinkable. The more power gained, the more important this principle becomes. Even our money benefits from a budget to tell it where to go. Otherwise, we wonder where it went.

The two greatest thieves of power are vibration and friction. They are also the chaotic killers in a person's life. Undisciplined rattling around builds friction between human will and the will of God and disintegrates the very soul. Holiness is called "the perfect law of liberty." Jesus declares that he came that his people might have life, and have it to the full. That's life with a capital L.

The Bible describes fully the joy of the life Jesus has provided. David says, "Delight yourself in the Lord and he will give you the desires of your heart" (Psalm 37:4). Peter explains in 1 Peter 1:8 that "inexpressible and glorious joy" are yours for the taking. John declares that God's purpose is to make your joy complete (1 John 1:4). Nehemiah prophesies that "the joy of the Lord is your strength" (Nehemiah 8:10). And Galatians 5:22 lists joy second only to love as a fruit of the Spirit.

When we lay everything on the altar, when we both trust and obey God, then our lives can be controlled by love and joy. In this are both the power and the bearings to transmit God's life to man's soul. This is the perfect law of liberty in action.

To fear this loving control is to fear life itself— abundant life. Man's rebellion against God's perfect will is cancer in the soul: "All who hate me love death" (Proverbs 8:36).

The God who gave us the Bible in the first place, by limiting unwanted motion and transmitting only his own wonderful words of life through the prophets; the God who came himself, fulfilling every jot and tittle of prophecy concerning himself in the fullness of time; this God, who runs the stars on time, knows both the power and the bearings necessary to carry out his will in the life of anyone.

To tamper with the terms is to court chaos and death. To trust and obey means love, life, joy and peace; such is the "glorious freedom of the children of God" (Romans 8:21).

The Secret

I met God in the morning
When the day was at its best,
And his presence came like sunrise
Like a glory in my breast.

All day long the presence lingered,
All day long he stayed with me;
And we sailed in perfect calmness
O'er a very troubled sea.

Other ships were blown and battered,
Other ships were sore distressed;
But the winds that seemed to drive them
Brought to us a peace and rest.

Then I thought of other mornings,
With a keen remorse of mind,
When I too, had loosed the moorings,
With his presence left behind.

So I think I know the secret
Learned from many a troubled way;
You must seek God in the morning
If you want him through the day.

Ralph S. Cushman

THE DIVING BELL

The diving bell is a perfect illustration of the spirit–filled life. This large, hollow apparatus is supplied with air through a hose, allowing persons in the bell to work underwater. As long as the air pressure inside the bell exceeds the water pressure outside, the water lies calm outside the shell, but if the air pressure leaks out, the water leaks in.

Likewise, if the pressure of the Holy Spirit's precious presence is in us, the world, the flesh and the devil stay out. Though all three are very much alive and well, they lie harmless and helpless under our feet. They cannot penetrate God's armor of righteousness and the shield of faith, which alone are 100 percent devil–proof. God says so in Ephesians 6:10–18.

Our fleshly susceptibility to sin does not actually die. We are commanded to "count" ourselves "dead to sin" (Romans 6:11). The old life of sin is to be a dead issue. As new creations, we are expected and enabled to turn a deaf ear to temptation.

But if, as Commissioner Samuel Logan Brengle warned, "we get so busy for God that time runs out, and we neglect our time with God," the love, the joy, the faith, the sense of call and guidance leak out, and pride sneaks in. We think we know what we are doing and that we can get along without his constant presence. Oh! how important it is to believe the words of Jesus, "Apart from me you can do nothing" (John 15:5).

Commissioner Brengle told my wife and me in our honeymoon corps that his temptations, as a sanctified man, had boiled down to one single issue: time with God. When he maintained it, as he had for the previous 30 years, all other temptations glanced off his shield of faith like water off a duck's back, but when he fell before this one temptation, as often happened in his early life, he instantly became vulnerable to ten thousand others. The only way he could avoid it was to make time with God his first priority.

He also found that by putting his Bible study first, before praying, it gave him cause to praise. He said, "I read until I get a blessing." It gave him "great and precious promises" (2 Peter 1:4). It gave him faith's only food (Romans 10:17 and 1 Peter 2:2). It gave him authority as he pled the promises in prayer.

We can live a holy life, but the holiness is his. Think of Galatians 2:20 as applying 220 volts to a dead motor: "I have been crucified with Christ and I no longer live, but Christ lives in me." When we are wholly his, our holy Lord furnishes the power to live a holy life. Therefore, we must give him all the glory.

Jesus purchased a complete salvation and enables us to be "more than conquerors through him who loved us" (Romans 8:37).

The kingdom of God is a kingdom of paradox,
where, through the ugly defeat of a cross, a holy God
is utterly glorified. Victory comes through defeat,
healing through brokenness, and finding self
through losing self.

Charles W. Colson

THREE
DIMENSIONAL
VISION

During World War II, the Vectograph was used for aerial reconnaissance because it could pierce all camouflage to take pictures.

It accomplished the task by taking simultaneous pictures through two cameras located on opposite wing tips of the plane. The pictures were taken through polaroid filters, the axis of one at a right angle to the other. They were developed as transparencies so one could be superimposed upon the other. Then they were studied through polarized glasses.

With these glasses, the right eye saw only what the camera had seen from its position on the right wing tip, and the left eye saw only what the other camera had seen from the opposite wing tip.

This three-dimensional perspective was of such accentuated heights and depths that no camouflage was effective against it. No longer could a tank or a parked plane be dressed up with chicken wire and wisps of hay to resemble a haystack.

By Vectograph a man's eyes were virtually 75 feet apart. Add telescopic lenses and infrared sensitive film, and you had human eyes that could pierce midnight darkness and impenetrable clouds with a clarity and acuteness of perception only attributed to Superman.

This is precisely what vital prayer life and feeding upon the word of God confers upon the believer. Perceptions are sharpened and extended literally "out of this world."

The eleventh chapter of Hebrews records the selfless lives and labors of heroes of old and comments, "the world was not worthy of them" (Hebrews 11:38). "All these people were still living by faith when they died. They did not receive the things promised; they only saw them and welcomed them from a distance. And they admitted that they were aliens and strangers on earth" (Hebrews 11:13).

Moses, crown prince of Egypt, "chose to be mistreated along with the people of God rather than to enjoy the pleasures of sin for a short time" (Hebrews 11:25). He did so by faith, regarding "disgrace for the sake of Christ as of greater value than the treasures of Egypt, because he was looking ahead to his reward ... he persevered because he saw him who is invisible" (Hebrews 11:26–27).

He saw what his critics could never see; he literally looked through God's eyes. Life was an open book. God's plans for the ages were open, and all of eternity lay before him as a clear panorama.

The youngest new believer, looking through God's eyes, beholds what the wisest philosopher without Christ can never guess exists. The Lord Jesus said: "I praise you, Father, Lord of heaven and earth, because you have hidden these things from the wise and learned, and revealed them to little children" (Matthew 11:25).

Any spiritual babe who will not cultivate a vital prayer life and establish the daily habit of feeding upon the word is "nearsighted and blind, and has forgotten that he has been cleansed from his past sins. Therefore, my brothers, be all the more eager to make your calling and election sure. For if you do these things, you will never fall" (2 Peter 1:9–10).

"For the word of God is living and active. Sharper than any double–edged sword, it penetrates even to dividing soul and spirit; it judges the thoughts and attitudes of the heart. Nothing in all creation is hidden from God's sight. Everything is uncovered and laid bare before the eyes of him to whom we must give account" (Hebrews 4:12–13).

There is always a moment of painful adjustment to the eyes in 3–D viewing. The eyes hurt for a few seconds as they struggle to resolve the conflict of what at first appears to be a double image.

Similarly, the paradoxes of Scripture appear at first sight to be contradictions. How can I lose my life by saving it? Or save my life by losing it? How can I have abundant life by crucifying the flesh, with its affections and lusts? How can I possess the Pearl of Greatest Price—the richest treasure in time or eternity—by counting every normal thing of value as loss for Christ? How can I have all things by losing all things and by considering them "rubbish, that I may gain Christ" (Philippians 3:8)?

This moment of painful adjustment, before the Lord's astonishing three–dimensional vision bursts upon us, discourages many Christians. That's why they never persevere in daily Bible searching or plead these promises in prayer until their lives become transfigured by the renewing of their minds. It's a painful process until the conflict is resolved and we yield to see things God's way, through his eyes.

Something in depraved human nature is reluctant to allow God to interfere with our lives. Unless we give our lives lock, stock and barrel to Christ, we lose them for eternity. John 6:48–66 records that 58 of our Lord's 70 disciples backslid from the very point at which they were called to holiness and refused to go all the way.

It's dangerous to say no to God at any level of the Christian walk. But if we say an eternal yes and resolve the painful paradox, we will see "him who is invisible" (Hebrews 11:27).

This is the life of holiness. To fear it or fall short of it is a profound insanity. To complicate the matter or make it mystical is to take personal credit for something that was wrought on Calvary and is the love gift of our Lord. As Wesley put it, "the Christian life is the life of God lived in these temples of clay, on the level of miracle." We were born again by merely touching the hem of his garment by faith. Let us touch him again as we look afresh at "great and precious promises, so that through them you may participate in the divine nature and escape the corruption in the world caused by evil desires" (2 Peter 1:4).

Holiness is his way—the way that sees all. There is no such thing as a half–way which confers half–sight, or three–quarters which confers a bit more. The only alternative to holiness is "turning back to those weak and miserable principles" and total blindness of the soul (Galatians 4:9).

Read again Hebrews 11 and 12 and note that nearly every form of the word "to see" in Greek is not *blepo*, or physical eyesight, but *horao*, to discern. This is the eyesight of the soul, God's own eyesight, available to us so we might truly see his perfection and our need of him, inherent in our imperfection.

Be patient! Look at the promises long enough, longingly enough, and the paradox will soon melt into the lovely features of the Lord. Then you will "with unveiled faces reflect the Lord's glory, being transformed into his likeness with ever–increasing glory, which comes from the Lord, who is the Spirit" (2 Corinthians 3:18).

"I have made you a light for the Gentiles, that
you may bring salvation to the ends of the earth."

Acts 13:47

THE MULTIPLICATION FACTOR

If a piece of paper six thousandths of an inch thick is folded in half 50 times, the result is a stack of paper 106,619,319 miles thick, reaching 13,000,000 miles beyond the sun. Of course, no human could fold any piece of paper—be it ever so large—even a dozen times, so great is the rate of increase.

This is the same rate at which germs multiply by cell division. This is the rate at which one rotten apple makes two, then four, then eight ... until the whole barrel is rotten. In the same way, one man tells a dirty story, then two tell it, until it travels around the world.

Chain letters nearly wrecked the U.S. postal system. The postmaster general had to plead with the nation to stop the fad.

The rate of multiplication, if unchecked, would soon wreck the universe if God had not built controls into the balance of nature. We've talked about it with the codfish, oysters and spawning sea hares. All of them lay eggs by the millions, but God's built-in controls keep the seas from being overrun by any one species.

The God of creation is a flawless mathematician. Everything works smoothly until man starts tampering with his checks and balances.

Remember how the saltwater lamprey destroyed the fishing industry once they were allowed to enter the Great Lakes? Or what about those American jack rabbits in Australia that the kangaroos wouldn't eat? Or the Arizona cactus that was brought in for fencing and took over the landscape?

Man is beyond his depth when he starts fooling with the balance of nature. Only the Creator's omniscience can see to the end from the beginning and perfectly provide for every creature, little or large, so that each can live and let live.

To pursue this principle of growth by multiplication instead of by addition, let us suppose that all of the 120 disciples in the upper room at Pentecost had backslidden but Peter. Let us also suppose that Peter had won only one convert in one year, instead of 3,000 in one day, and that they had continued to win just one each year. The present population of the earth would have been saved in less than 33 years!

If the world today had a million born-again Christians on fire for the Lord, the world would be at the feet of Christ in 12 years. But, of course, the gospel is not unopposed, and not all converts are fertile. Most are sterile, incapable of reproduction or at least unwilling to obey the Great Commission of Matthew 28:19–20. The world's birthrate is fast outrunning the beautiful feet of the publishers of peace. The world can never be fully evangelized unless it is accomplished in a single generation, but this can only be accomplished by a hardier breed of believer patterned after Pentecost.

How effectively Satan can block revival by fostering professional jealousy and getting us to employ human yardsticks of success in soul winning, which lulls us to sleep in the midst of fields "white unto the harvest" (John 4:35). How effectively the fear of man can paralyze one's word of witness!

All need not be gifted in word and deed like Peter, but all need a personal encounter with the risen Lord; a sense of urgency in the light of his imminent return and a heart set aflame by the Holy Spirit to drive them to exploits of love like Andrew. We have no record of Andrew's preaching, but we do have a record of his reaching. He brought his brother Peter to Jesus.

We are not all preachers, but God can make us all reachers. Then we can expect the promised fire–storm of revival to sweep the earth in our time.

"Stand firm, then, with the belt of truth buckled

around your waist, with the breastplate of righteousness in place, and with your feet fitted with the readiness that comes from the gospel of peace. In addition to all this, take up the shield of faith, with which you can extinguish all the flaming arrows of the evil one. Take the helmet of salvation and the sword of the Spirit, which is the word of God. And pray in the Spirit on all occasions with all kinds of prayers and requests" (Ephesians 6:14–18).

When Jesus cried, "It is finished," he did not take away the conflict, the contest, the fight. No! He took away only your defeat.

Ira Taylor

THE BOMBARDIER
& THE SOLE

The bombardier beetle is just a little fellow, but bullies should beware, because he is armed to the teeth, or should I say, to the tail.

A German chemist named Hermann Schildnecht discovered that this little critter possesses two cannons. Its arsenal consists of two explosive chemicals, hydrogen peroxide and hydroquinon; an inhibitor to keep them from exploding; an anti–inhibitor that instantly counteracts the inhibitor to trigger the explosion; two storage chambers; two combustion chambers; and a communication network.

All of these systems have to be in flawless working condition for the beetle to survive. The cannons without the explosives would be meaningless. One chemical without the other would not explode. Both chemicals, without the inhibitor, would blow the beetle to bits. Without the anti–inhibitor, the beetle would be unable to trigger the explosion at all. Without the storage chambers, it wouldn't have the chemicals on hand when needed. Without strongly reinforced, heat–proof combustion tubes and cannons, the heat generated by the explosion would cook the beetle.

But most amazing of all is the hair trigger communications system. The beetle identifies a potential enemy; waits until the enemy gets its mouth open; pulls the anti–inhibitor like a firing pin on a rifle; aims its cannons; and sends a scalding blast of noxious gas from its tail into the mouth of the aggressor, curbing its appetite for any more beetles. These five functions must be perfectly timed to a fraction of a second.

If God takes such minute care of beetles, his word in Philippians 4:19 is a mighty comfort: "My God will meet all your needs according to his glorious riches in Christ Jesus." So is verse 7 of the same chapter: "And the peace of God, which transcends all understanding, will guard your hearts and your minds in Christ Jesus."

His blood has purchased all the equipment we need to have daily victory over the world, the flesh and the devil. "Therefore put on the full armor of God, so that when the day of evil comes, you may be able to stand your ground, and after you have done everything, to stand" (Ephesians 6:13).

A variety of a little flat fish found in the Red Sea, called the sole, is also equipped with a marvelous safety device against predators. This device was observed at Sea World, where the smaller fish were displayed in the same tank with a shark.

Ordinarily, the shark didn't attack little fish as long as it was kept well–fed. But one day, the shark bolted after a sole with its great mouth wide open. As the keepers looked on, the shark just kept its mouth open, letting the sole escape, and wagging its head as if in disappointment. After the shark was able to close its mouth, it went after the sole again, with the same result. It seemed to be stricken suddenly with lockjaw.

The guards wondered if the sole had somehow paralyzed the shark long enough to escape. They washed the sole in alcohol to remove any poison it might have emitted. This time the shark gobbled up the sole without any difficulty. Upon examination of another sole, they discovered about a dozen little jets around the outside edge of the fish that eject a paralyzing toxin. They also found that the sole is equipped with an immunity system against the toxin.

Only God could have fashioned the sole's protective system. God has given believers a protective armor too. Described in Ephesians 6:10–18, it is 100 percent devil–proof. See especially verse 16: "Take up the shield of faith, with which you can extinguish all the flaming arrows of the evil one."

Again, 1 Corinthians 10:13 gives us the encouraging truth: "No temptation has seized you except what is common to man. And God is faithful; he will not let you be tempted beyond what you can bear. But when you are tempted, he will also provide a way out so that you can stand up under it."

And we won't need twelve jets to shoot out our protection. We only need use the shield of faith, faith in his word. Jesus is our example. He was tempted in the wilderness three times. There are only three basic temptations, "the cravings of sinful man, the lust of his eyes and the boasting of what he has and does" (1 John 2:16–17). Jesus was tempted by all three, but deflected each deadly dart with his shield, quoting God's word.

Note finally, in 2 Peter 1:4–10, this passage begins with "great and precious promises," and ends with "you will never fall." Let's hide his word in our hearts, so that we will not sin against him.

In the love of Jesus I have found a refuge,
Though the winds may blow, this one thing I know,
He who never faileth is my shield and shelter,
And he leads me where still waters flow;
He leads me where still waters flow.

Sidney Edward Cox

SHEEP & SHEPHERDS

Sheep seem to be the only animals that don't know their way home. Actually, they don't have a home. Sheep were evidently created to be domesticated, as they have been from the time of Cain and Abel, according to Genesis 4:2.

Whenever a creature is created with some apparent handicap, God endows it with some extra or intensified faculty. While sheep have no sense of direction, they do have fantastic hearing. If a lamb has been born with a certain shepherd, it will forever afterwards recognize that shepherd's voice.

If a hundred shepherds were all calling their sheep at the same time, each sheep would go to its own shepherd. But if sheep are terrorized by some predator, and the shepherd isn't around to calm them, they would scatter and get lost. This is why shepherds in the Near East live with their sheep day and night. Their only sheep cote, or shelter, is an occasional enclosure of field stone. This is a low wall about three feet high without a gate—just an opening. The shepherd lies down across the six foot opening and acts as the door. Thus the picture of Jesus as the good shepherd and the door for the sheep was readily understood by the Jews of his day.

Another advantage sheep have is that they tend to huddle or flock. God implanted the instinct to huddle in many creatures as an effective means of protection. No bat will fly into a cloud of insects; no lion will go into a herd of gazelles; no barracuda will swim into a school of fish; no hawk will fly into a dense flock of migrating birds. Predators only pick off the strays.

God also wants believers to huddle—in flocks called churches and corps. Hebrews 10:25 instructs us to "not give up meeting together, as some are in the habit of doing, but let us encourage one another—and all the more as you see the day approaching."

A predator of sheep tries to break a flock before attacking individuals. A dog will run up and down the side of a flock to create panic. Satan uses the same strategy. He tries to split a congregation by getting members to gossip about or resent one another.

That's why Jesus prayed, "I have given them the

glory that you gave me, that they may be one as we are one: I in them and you in me. May they be brought to complete unity to let the world know that you sent me and have loved them even as you have loved me ... I have made you known to them, and will continue to make you known in order that the love you have for me may be in them and that I myself may be in them" (John 17:22–23,26).

I believe that the number one responsibility of a pastor or corps officer is to keep his flock loving one another and to reconcile factions quickly. Jesus made it crystal clear that we must forgive to be forgiven (see Matthew 5:23–24, 5:41–45, 6:14–15, 18:23–35 and Mark 11:25–26). This is vitally important.

People are like sheep in many ways. Isaiah 53:6 says, "We all, like sheep, have gone astray, each of us has turned to his own way; and the Lord has laid on him the iniquity of us all." Jeremiah tells us, "I know, O Lord, that a man's life is not his own; it is not for man to direct his steps" (Jeremiah 10:23). And "There is a way that seems right to a man, but in the end it leads to death" (Proverbs 14:12).

People, like sheep, have no innate sense of direction. *We need the Good Shepherd to guide us safely through life to heaven.* Without him, we are lost.

"May the God of peace, who through the blood of the eternal covenant brought back from the dead our Lord Jesus, that great Shepherd of the sheep, equip you with everything good for doing his will, and may he work in us what is pleasing to him, through Jesus Christ, to whom be glory for ever and ever. Amen" (Hebrews 13:20–21).

I'm in His Hands

I shall not fear though darkened clouds
may gather 'round me.
The God I serve is one
who cares and understands.
Although the storms I face
would threaten to confound me,
of this I am assured: I'm in his hands!

What though I cannot know
the way that lies before me,
I still can trust and freely
follow his commands.
My faith is firm since
he it is who watches o'er me.
Of this I'm confident: I'm in his hands!

In days gone by my Lord
has always proved sufficient,
when I have yielded to the
law of love's demands.
Why should I doubt that he
will evermore be present
to make his will my own?
I'm in his hands!

Stanley E. Ditmer

IN HIS HANDS

The human hand is amazing. It can be used to create, heal, comfort, support and guide.

Watch a concert pianist's fingers flying across the keys and hear the gorgeous music. Watch an artist at the easel. After his hands have finished, a beautiful picture emerges from splotches of paint. Watch a surgeon, with steady-handed precision, work to save a life. No other part of God's creation can do such things.

It is no wonder the Bible uses the image of the hands and fingers of God to describe the ease with which he does such mighty works (Luke 11:20; Psalm 8:3–9). *The hand of God is used to describe the unerring skill and power ascribed to him.*

There is also power in the gentleness of touch. The

touch of a mother's hand sends a thrill through a child's body. Even when we are old, we get great comfort from our dear ones holding our hands.

In India, the child of a leper, even a child with no trace of the disease, will never be touched by his playmates. It is cruel rejection and total isolation. Yet when a leper came to Jesus and said, "'Lord, if you are willing, you can make me clean.' Jesus reached out his hand and touched the man. 'I am willing,' he said. 'Be clean!' Immediately he was cured of his leprosy" (Matthew 8:2–3).

It wasn't that Jesus needed to touch him, for on another occasion when ten lepers stood far off and cried to him, he just gave them a word of command: "'Go, show yourselves to the priests.' And as they went, they were cleansed" (Luke 17:14). In times of illness and when death approaches, even the strongest man is glad to know that God will "hold me by my right hand. You guide me with your counsel, and afterward you will take me into glory" (Psalm 73:23–24).

When Commissioner Stanley E. Ditmer (R) wrote the song "I'm in His Hands," he was gravely ill, and the song is a testament to how God cradles his loved ones, even through the darkest periods. Ditmer relates:

The question keeps coming to me: What were the circumstances behind the writing of my song, "I'm in His Hands"? Apparently, several versions have been given. A clarification of this deeply moving spiritual experience has, therefore, been requested.

During the time I was stationed at the School for Officers' Training in New York City, I was with a brigade of cadets on a ten–day campaign in April 1956. I was summoned to Philadelphia, where my brother was seriously ill.

One month later I also became ill. The doctors were unable to diagnose the cause. It was a time of uncertainty and great concern.

It was during this period that "I'm in His Hands" was born. It was not "written," it simply "evolved" at the piano keyboard one morning. Then I laid it aside and soon forgot it.

Six months later much had changed. My illness had been diagnosed; I was better; my brother was alive; and my wife and I were corps officers.

When my wife and I were asked to sing a duet for our annual officers' retreat, the memory of the verse and chorus came to me. I thought this would be an appropriate selection, so I found the copy and wrote what is now the third verse.

After its introduction, the officers sang the chorus repeatedly. Many requests for copies came, so I wrote another verse and sent it to *The War Cry,* and thus it began its journey around the Army world.

Although it was born at a time of sickness and death, it was not conceived by me in that manner, but as an expression of virile faith and courage.

How wonderful to know "My times are in your hands" (Psalm 31:15). The God of all comfort says, "Can a mother forget the baby at her breast and have no compassion on the child she has borne? Though she may forget, I will not forget you! See, I have engraved you on the palms of my hands; your walls are ever before me" (Isaiah 49:15–16).

PART III:

MARKS OF THE SPIRIT'S SHARP SWORD

The well is deep and I require
A draught of the water of life,
But none can quench my soul's desire
For a draught of the water of life;
Till one draws near who the cry will heed,
Helper of men in their time of need,
And I, believing, find indeed
That Christ is the water of life.

Albert Orsborn

TOO LITTLE,
TOO LATE

During our family devotionals, we often spent time researching answers from God's word, with the children our most challenging audience. No questions were barred as unimportant. If we could not answer them at once, the questions were tabled until we could answer them. This made the family altar exciting and highly anticipated.

Many brokenhearted parents cry out in bewilderment: "How could it happen? I raised my child to be a good Christian, but now he won't go near church. He claims he had too much religion as a boy. What went wrong? Did I overdo it?"

It is possible for a child to have too much program. There is danger when feet run faster than faith. But no one can have too much salvation. We need to exhibit in ourselves, and expect of our children, a 100 percent surrender to the will of God. One speck less is madness.

Another parental cry is: "How does it happen that one child is a delightful Christian, while another is utterly godless? They had the same parents, the same church, the same family altar. What did I do wrong?"

The simple answer is that the first child became genuinely converted, while the second child did not. The first child had the power of God to help him live the victorious life. The second child was on his own, with neither power nor inclination to do the will of God.

If a mosquito receives less than a lethal dose of DDT, its offspring will be resistant to a more concentrated dose. Each successive generation exposed but not killed becomes more and more immune, until a 100 percent solution would not kill them.

Staphylococcus germs found in common pus are easily killed by minute doses of penicillin. But if they are on the fringe of things and exposed to the drug in less than lethal concentrations, staph becomes a veritable monster that no amount of penicillin can kill. Sadly, Staph infection once wiped out the entire nursery of a New York hospital, as the penicillin came too little, too late.

To inform a child's mind without changing his heart can actually make him resistant to the gospel. Children often put on an act to keep from being nagged by their parents. They go through the motions. They say the right words; they appear to be saved, but the whole hypocritical pretense finally nauseates them. Outward conformity without inward grace soon tears a person to pieces. Little wonder that they chuck the whole thing when they move out of the home and are on their own.

The antidote is very simple: make sure the child is soundly converted and growing in grace. *One cannot live the Christian life without Christ.*

Even a saved child, if he refuses to go on to the Spirit–filled life and the joy unspeakable it produces, gets a feeling that Christianity is a series of negatives and a bundle of joy–killing prohibitions. Everything he calls fun, his parents call sinful. He doesn't have the joy of the Lord; he dare not indulge in the fun of the devil. He has just enough religion to keep him miserable.

Steady growth in grace produces the fruit of the Spirit: love, joy, peace and other qualities listed in Galatians 5:22–23, but some children hit a plateau past which they refuse to grow. God calls them to higher heights, but they become disobedient and grow "ineffective and unproductive" (2 Peter 1:8). Second Peter 1:9 states, "But if anyone does not have (the fruits of the Spirit), he is nearsighted and blind, and has forgotten that he has been cleansed from his past sins." To keep up a front, therefore, only increases this blindness.

Sightless eyes of unbelief can see nothing attractive about God or the church. If you become aware of this attitude developing in your children, check quickly into their devotional life. Some plants look dead, when all they need is a little watering. It takes roots to produce fruit, and roots need water—the water of the word. Others are really dead, "without fruit and uprooted—twice dead" (Jude 1:2).

The parable of the sower in Luke 8 shows that the seed, God's word, is the same in all four cases. The difference is in the soil. We, as parents, have a part to play in the preparation and cultivation of that soil, our children's hearts and minds.

Parents who profess faith but possess nothing can transmit nothing to their children. Other parents, who may personally make it through to heaven, can, by their unbridled tongue and unsanctified temper, actually destroy their children spiritually. The child may later claim to have had too much religion as a boy, when the problem really was that he saw too little for it to be attractive and saw it too late to be effective. So he feels it is all a sad exaggeration and not for him.

It is possible, too, for the godliest of parents to mistake their little crows for swans. Some can never see anything wrong with their offspring. They can believe in the doctrine of new birth, yet act as though children could sop up salvation by osmosis. They waste time and energy making their children measure up to external standards of conduct, when the basic problem is inward backsliding that goes unchallenged.

Thank God, there are parents who are filled with the joy of the Lord and are determined to share that faith daily with their children, making them a vital part of the exciting adventure of living for Jesus.

Parents can wait too long in challenging their children. It is not necessary for youth to have lost years, sowing wild oats. Jesus can satisfy youth. After all, "His divine power has given us everything we need for life and godliness" (2 Peter 1:3).

If you want boldness, take part in the fight;
If you want purity, walk in the light;
If you want liberty, shout and be free;
Enjoying a full salvation.

George Phippen Ewens

A LOBSTER'S DEFENSE

The lobster has weird equipment. As author David Egner points out, "It runs backward; hears with its legs; tastes with its feet; chews its food with teeth in its stomach; and, because the lobster is delicious food for other sea creatures, the Lord gave it a full suit of armor" (*Our Daily Bread*, July 21, 1989).

A lobster may look crazy, but, upon analysis, its odd equipment is very purposeful. For instance, if a lobster turned around to run away, a predator could whack off its tasty tail, and it is a much more formidable opponent facing an enemy with its threatening claws as it backs out of trouble.

Lobsters hear by hydrophones in their legs. They can hear the flip of a tail or the wiggle of a worm. And since they live down on the murky bottom all their lives, the handiest way for them to taste potential food is through their feet. They can also bolt their food and chew it later with the teeth in their stomach.

It is very functional to have their eyes on stalks; they can get a good look at things, but if they are threatened, they can retract their eyes as they back out of danger.

Mama lobster lays about 3,000 eggs at a time. The moment the babies hatch, they can swim freely and are soon on their own. Many enemies prey upon the babies, but enough survive to propagate the next generation and supply the enormous demand of gourmet restaurants, their chief adversaries.

A lobster's best defense is his armor. Form–fitting, hard plastic plates overlay his entire body.

The Christian's only defense is the spiritual armor described in Ephesians 6:10–18. As we look at it, piece by piece, we discover that each part fulfills a different function of God's word in a believer's life and warfare. No wonder we are commanded to "put on the full armor of God so that you can take your stand against the devil's schemes" (Ephesians 6:11).

The belt of truth: "Your word is truth" (John 17:17).

The breastplate of righteousness: "All your commands are righteousness" (Psalm 119:172).

Feet fitted with the readiness that comes from the gospel of peace: "Your word is a lamp to my feet and a light for my path" (Psalm 119:105).

The shield of faith: "This is the victory that has overcome the world, even our faith" (1 John 5:4).

The helmet of salvation: "Be transformed by the renewing of your mind" (Romans 12:2).

The sword of the Spirit: "Which is the word of God" (Ephesians 6:17).

Prayer in the Spirit on all occasions: "Pray continually" (1 Thessalonians 5:17).

God never intended us to live defeated lives. Calvary has given us the equipment to be "more than conquerors through him that loved us" (Romans 8:37).

Without Jesus, the Living Word, and his written word, there is no knowing. We should meditate on it day and night. Without Jesus, there is no going. Dr. Bob Cook said, "We must put feet under our faith." Without Jesus, there is no showing. We would have no message, no witness. Without Jesus, there is no growing. "Like newborn babies, crave pure spiritual milk, so that by it you may grow up in your salvation, now that you have tasted that the Lord is good" (1 Peter 2:2–3).

In short, the Bible is the only food for faith. Romans 10:17 reminds us that "faith comes from hearing the message, and the message is heard through the word of Christ." It is our only defense against temptation, our only offensive weapon, and our only standard of conduct. It is light upon our path, our title deed to Glory and the compass pointing to our destination.

Give us a pure heart that we may see Thee;
A humble heart that we may hear Thee;
A heart of love that we may serve Thee;
A heart of faith that we may live Thee.

Dag Hammarskjöld

An Owl's
Special
Apparatus

verything about owls seems to be different from other birds. They are uniquely formed for their special niche in the balance of nature.

The ring–necked pheasant, with wing feathers that are stiff and sturdy, stirs up a lot of sound and fury when it takes off. It explodes from the ground like a whirlwind; thus pheasants are also called thunderbirds.

In contrast, an owl's pinions taper to a soft, velvety fringe, and its wings are so large and the beat so slow that there is not the faintest whisper as it glides in for the attack.

Its eyeballs don't move, but they are so huge that an owl can see clearly in a hundredth of the light required by humans. These frozen eyeballs are a distinct advantage to the owl, as it unerringly zeroes in on its prey. Also the eyes are widely separated for binocular vision.

However, immovable eyeballs severely limit the owl's breadth of field. To compensate for this, the Creator gave owls additional vertebrae in their necks, allowing them to swivel their heads 270 degrees. This way they can turn their heads left and look directly behind them—or keep going to have a look over their right shoulder.

Humans can scarcely turn their heads 45 degrees. Of course, they can roll their eyes another 45 degrees, and they can swing their shoulders another 45 degrees. Even so, an owl's neck is twice as flexible.

The owl's hearing is as fantastic as its sight. Some species have huge ears hidden under their feathers, with the right ear pointed up and the left ear pointed down. This gives them stereo hearing of great accuracy, with which they can pinpoint the origin of a tiny squeak of a mouse under a leaf.

Another peculiarity of owls is their ability to gulp their prey down whole—fur, fins, feathers, bones, teeth and talons. Then right in their stomachs they sort out the hard stuff, which they can't digest, wrap it in fur, and cough it up. One can locate an owl's roost by these owl balls at the foot of the tree where they roost by day.

We as humans, created in the image of God, may not have all the owl's special equipment, but we have superior gifts of grace.

We won't need wings, because whether we die in Christ or live to meet him at the rapture, "the dead in Christ will rise first. After that, we who are still alive and are left will be caught up together with them in the clouds to meet the Lord in the air. And so we will be with the Lord forever" (1 Thessalonians 4:16–17).

We have better vision than the owl; we can, with the eyes of faith, see "him who is invisible" (Hebrews 11:27). "For what is seen is temporary, but what is unseen is eternal" (2 Corinthians 4:18).

We might not be able to turn our necks 270 degrees, but Jesus said that every willing sinner can repent and turn "from darkness to light, and from the power of Satan to God, so that they may receive forgiveness of sins and a place among those who are sanctified by faith in me" (Acts 26:18).

We don't need the super hearing of owls. Every human—even the deaf—can hear the word of Jesus in the scriptural sense, because the word translated here in John 5:24 means not only to get the message, but to do something about it. Our Southern neighbors have it right, as when a mother tells her little boy to do something, then adds, "Ya' heah?" This means gut–deep comprehension and a heart willing to obey.

We don't need special apparatus to cough up owl balls. We are admonished, instead, not to swallow "every wind of teaching" (Ephesians 4:14).

God gave owls everything they need to take their

particular place in nature. *Likewise, God gives us everything we need to take our particular place in the body of Christ.* Ephesians 4:15–16 explains, if we do not swallow "every wind of teaching," but, speak "truth in love, we will in all things grow up into him who is the head, that is Christ. From him the whole body, joined and held together by every supporting ligament, grows and builds itself up in love, as each part does its work."

**You don't have to see God to know him.
Faith, which works by love, can see in the dark.**

Lyell Rader

SEEING
THE INVISIBLE

E normous scientific interest has been generated over the last several decades by remote sensing. Photographs and other evidence from space help us find fish, locate oil, minerals and water, reduce disease in crops and forests and predict crop yields worldwide to better prevent famine.

Rain forests, with perpetual impenetrable cloud cover, can be accurately mapped by a type of photography called side–looking radar, which cuts through midnight darkness, fog or smog, generating a three dimensional picture as clear as if it had been taken at noon on the brightest day.

Radio signals beamed down on Antarctica's Nimrod

Glacier in 1967 enabled British scientists to map not just the top, but also the underside of the 3,000–foot ice and note whether it rested on land or water. The technique involved reading and recording the echoes similar to a bat's echolocation mechanism.

Infrared photographs taken from the air can detect where a car had been parked or where a plane had taken off a full hour earlier. The resulting photo reveals the vehicle's silhouette.

Such photographs taken from low–flying aircraft can penetrate the densest jungle at night and spot a single man or beast hiding in the bushes. Different temperatures are recorded in the picture as different colors. A bare arm or face would photograph red. Body warmth coming through clothing would look yellow. Trees and brush would look green, while the still cooler ground would look blue or black. This technique was used by American forces in Vietnam.

The historic picture of a bearded prospector leading his donkey up into "them thar hills" is outmoded. Modern geologists can merely fly over the hills, and, with gamma ray photography, analyze the chemical content of the soil and rocks, which is particularly useful in locating radioactive minerals such as uranium, potassium and thorium.

It is possible to fly over a field of wheat and detect the presence of the grain disease "black–stem rust" long before its discovery by someone on the ground.

Equipment used by forest rangers from a plane 20,000 feet in the air can detect a fire that has just started.

One look at man's sophisticated remote–sensing equipment and anyone can realize that it represents untold hours of research by brilliant men and women of science. Such design demands a designer. Devices like these just couldn't occur by accident.

God has been in the remote–sensing business since the dawn of creation. Bionomicists have discovered more than 500 varieties of marine life that possess remote–sensing organs. The electric eel, for instance, can distinguish prey from predator through the murky waters of the Amazon River from a distance of 40 feet.

Every part of the body of the common catfish, from whiskers to tail, is vibrant with remote–sensing equipment. It can detect every flip of a tail, wiggle of a worm, flutter of an insect and even the backwash from motionless obstacles.

Pit vipers get the same type of picture of their prey as an infrared camera, plus x–ray. They can distinguish depth and avoid areas where bone is near the surface. As for spotting fires at a distance, rattlesnakes can detect even lukewarm temperatures to within one thousandth of one degree Fahrenheit.

Human beings also possess a functioning remote sense, called conscience, with which we feebly grope after God. While we know that life doesn't always ring true, that we are capable of grevious wrongdoing, we struggle in vain to escape our darkest dreams and fears.

But what glorious news we have to declare, for no one, since Calvary, has needed to grope. The great Creator has become our Savior. He did all the reaching when he laid aside his glory and came to this earth to seek and to save what was lost. He offers us his nail–scarred hand not to grope after, but to grip.

We don't have to see him to know him. Faith, expressing itself through love, can see in the dark. It is said of Moses that he "persevered because he saw him who is invisible" (Hebrews 11:27). We can do the same because, as St. Paul declares, "we live by faith, not by sight" (2 Corinthians 5:7).

**Stand against that which is wrong;
show why it is wrong; overcome it;
and plant truth in its place.**

A. W. Tozer

TENDER LIPS & SCALDED STOMACHS

wo experienced carpenters always greeted each other with a particular salutation: "welcome to the stub club." The first had lost a finger; the other had lost a thumb—after nearly 50 years of combined experience with buzz saws. Are there no guards, no safety devices for power saws? Surely! But who uses them?

There is a gambler's instinct in everyone which says, "Accidents happen to the other fellow."

God has built amazing safety devices into our bodies. For example, our fingers are far more sensitive to heat than our tender lips; our lips can be burned with a temperature our throats can stand; and our throats can be burned with a temperature our stomachs can take. So what do we do? We put handles on cups to avoid the first warning; make cups of plastic or porcelain to avoid the second; gulp down the tea to avoid the third; and still scald our insides.

We do exactly the same thing in moral matters.

Who heeds the warnings of the conscience or the written word of God thundering against sin? If enough people can be persuaded to do something, that makes it legal in the minds of the mob. History is replete with examples of the consequences when mass mentality takes over.

But majority opinion will never move Almighty God in his judgments. The laws of eternal life and of eternal banishment from his presence are as plain as print can make them. The bleeding body of God the Son still blocks the path to hell. The feeble voice of conscience still cries out against sin, in spite of mob approval. Contrary to majority opinion that eternal life is for "squares" only, God says whosoever will, may come.

John Wesley once warned, "If you are traveling in the direction of the generality of man, make sure of this: you are heading for the pit."

We speak of margins of safety. But the widest of margins are too narrow for comfort. Margins—either narrow or wide—are for gamblers. Why gamble when you can be sure? The Way of Life is a way of certainty and safety which Jesus trod before us. The Narrow Way is as safe as the throne of God.

Christ satisfies the mind as well as the heart: "You

will seek me and find me when you seek me with all your heart. 'I will be found by you,' declares the Lord" (Jeremiah 29:13,14). And the Psalmist says, "Taste and see that the Lord is good; blessed is the man who takes refuge in him" (Psalm 34:8).

When Peter wrote his second epistle, he recalled the wonder of the Mount of Transfiguration, where he and his fellow disciples saw firsthand that Jesus' "face shone like the sun, and his clothes became as white as the light. [And] there appeared before them Moses and Elijah, talking with Jesus. Peter said to Jesus, 'Lord, it is good for us to be here. If you wish, I will put up three shelters—one for you, one for Moses and one for Elijah.' While he was still speaking, a bright cloud enveloped them, and a voice from the cloud said, 'This is my Son, whom I love; with him I am well pleased. Listen to him!'" (Matthew 17:2–5).

Some would think that no experience could equal that. Yet 2 Peter 1:19–21 says, "And we have the word of the prophets made more certain, and you will do well to pay attention to it, as to a light shining in a dark place, until the day dawns and the morning star rises in your hearts. Above all, you must understand that no prophecy of Scripture came about by the prophet's own interpretation. For prophecy never had its origin in the will of man, but men spoke from God as they were carried along by the Holy Spirit."

In other words, the Bible is more sure even than the

Transfiguration! Peter experienced that, yet he backslid. He felt the strong hands of Jesus wash his feet in the upper room, yet within a few hours, he denied his Lord not once, but three times.

The Bible is "the out breathing of God." (See Robert L. Saucy's *The Bible Breathed from God*, Victor Books.) It is our only authority for getting to heaven and our only authority for living the Christ life, here and now.

The great white throne of judgment will not judge men by the opinions of the critics, but by "the word of His power" (Hebrews 1:3). We'd better believe it, know it and walk in its light by obedient faith. Let us teach our children early that it is "not as the word of men, but as it actually is, the word of God, which is at work in you who believe" (1 Thessalonians 2:13).

Engraved as in eternal brass
The mighty promise shines;
Nor can the powers of darkness raze
Those everlasting lines.

His very word of grace is strong
As that which built the skies;
The voice that rolls the stars along
Speaks all the promises.

My hiding place, my refuge tower,
And shield, art thou, O Lord;
I firmly anchor all my hopes
On thy unerring word.

J. I. Packer

SIMPLE RULES FOR STAYING ALIVE

The hardest thing for most Christians to maintain is a steadfast personal altar. Next to that comes maintaining an effective family altar. It has always been so, for the simple reason that all hell is out to stop the child of God from vital contact with his Lord. There are mechanical difficulties, like shift work that alters parents' routine, or staggered school hours that make it difficult to get all the children together at any one time. Surely, young parents today have problems my generation never had to face.

The basic problem is definitely spiritual: "We are not fighting against people made of flesh and blood, but against persons without bodies—the evil rulers of the unseen world, those mighty satanic beings and great evil princes of darkness who rule this world; and against huge numbers of wicked spirits in the spirit world" (Ephesians 6:12, TLB).

We cannot squeeze a 25th hour into the 24 we have been given each day. Our only hope, therefore, is to rearrange priorities on the divine pattern, with motivation born of God's command. A high priority is not enough; it must be first.

As we have seen earlier, prayer is a Christian's breath, Bible study a Christian's food, and obedience a Christian's exercise.

Satan is too intelligent and too guileful an adversary to tempt a sensitive Christian to stop praying abruptly; that would be far too obvious. His favorite method is to put the pressure on gradually to make one busier and busier for God, until there is neither time nor energy left to spend time with God. He lashes our conscience, driving us to accomplish by sweat what can be done "'not by might nor by power, but by my Spirit,' says the Lord Almighty" (Zechariah 4:6).

Manna was the only food that sustained ancient Israel during their 40–year sojourn between Egypt and the Promised Land. What a balanced diet! What preventive medicine! According to Scripture, none of the horrible diseases of Egypt hit them: "From among their tribes no one faltered" (Psalm 105:37).

There was just one catch. They had to gather manna fresh every morning, or it "was full of maggots and began to smell" (Exodus 16:20). There was one exception. Twice as much fell on the sixth day, while none fell on the Sabbath.

In spite of God's faithfulness in providing this miracle food this way for forty years, Israel was a long time coming to the conclusion that God said what he meant and meant what he said. Christians can be thick–headed on this matter too.

Most of us learn the hard way that Jesus was allowing no exceptions when he said, "Apart from me you can do nothing" (John 15:5). But abiding in him is fruitful beyond imagination. Jesus said, "If you remain in me and my words remain in you, ask whatever you wish, and it will be given you" (John 15:7).

One of the most amazingly complex mechanisms of the human body is its immunology. This is the ability to detect an enemy intruder and quickly manufacture the exact chemical compound, called antibodies, needed to destroy it. Immunology is often referred to as "the astonishing wisdom of the body." Of course, the believer is not at all astonished that his Creator, in infinite wisdom, should have thus programmed his body. These processes go on automatically, independent of one's conscious mind or control.

A nursing baby, for example, absorbs much more than simple nourishment from its mother's milk. It receives the mother's antibodies as well. Every disease a mother has had in her lifetime has produced these antibodies, which are then passed on to the child. The cleverest formula we can create through science still cannot compete with God's natural provision.

Paul commands us, "Like newborn babies, crave pure spiritual milk, so that by it you may grow up in your salvation, now that you have tasted that the Lord is good" (1 Peter 2:2–3). Here we have real soul food, of which God's marvelous manna is the type. Any spiritual babe, nursing upon this milk of the word, receives the very antibodies of Christ himself, who "has been tempted in every way, just as we are—yet was without sin" (Hebrews 4:15).

Feeding on God's word daily thus confers on the believer a 100 percent immunity against Satan's wiles: "No weapon forged against you will prevail" (Isaiah 54:17). "In addition to all this, take up the shield of faith, with which you can extinguish all the flaming arrows of the evil one" (Ephesians 6:16).

Have you noticed that doctors are reluctant to make 100 percent claims for any one medicine or procedure? They are wise to exercise such caution. But God is not hesitant or reserved in making the boldest 100 percent guarantees, such as, "if you do these things, you will never fall" (2 Peter 1:10).

Let us not tamper with this command of our omniscient God. We cannot outsmart him. Compromise at this point is lethal. We must keep eating the word, keep breathing prayer, and keep exercising glad obedience.

Prayer was our Lord's first priority. It must be ours! If we want to obey God desperately, we somehow will be able to get the family to pray together and stay together. Love will find a way, and our mighty Lord stands ready to make it work.